D1760996

BEYOND
WORDS

BEYOND WORDS

DZOGCHEN
MADE SIMPLE

Julia Lawless and Judith Allan

Dedicated with profound gratitude to our precious teacher
Chögyal Namkhai Norbu

Element
An Imprint of HarperCollins*Publishers*
77–85 Fulham Palace Road
Hammersmith, London W6 8JB

The website address is: www.thorsonselement.com

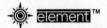

and *Element* are trademarks of
HarperCollins*Publishers* Limited

Published by Element 2003

A catalogue record for this book
is available from the British Library

ISBN 0 00 711677 2

Printed and bound in Great Britain by
Creative Print and Design (Wales), Ebbw Vale

CONTENTS

PLATE ILLUSTRATIONS

FOREWORD

It is not very easy to give a brief introduction to Dzogchen because it is a very ancient teaching which has developed over many centuries. This means that there is a lot to learn. But if we go to the essential principles of the Dzogchen teachings, then maybe I can give you some idea of what Dzogchen really means.

We speak of 'the Dzogchen teachings', but the actual meaning of the term *Dzogchen* is 'knowledge of the individual's real condition'. *Dzogchen* is a Tibetan word: *dzog* means 'the perfected state'; *chen* means 'total'. The total perfected state is our potentiality. So each person has their own Dzogchen, their own potentiality – and not only human beings, but all sentient beings. And in order to discover our potentiality, we have teachings.

Why do we need teachings to discover our potentiality? Because our real nature or potentiality is considered something beyond words, judgement or intellectual analysis. Even if we studied for years, we would not arrive at this state of knowledge and understanding. This applies not only to Dzogchen, but to Buddhist teachings in general. Through words alone, it is difficult to enter into real knowledge. In order to enter into real knowledge, we need experience. Experience is related to the teachings and methods. The teachings are taught by those who have realization of that knowledge, and they pass on their experience. In giving teachings, the teacher not only has to convince the student but also to open their eyes so they can discover their real nature or potentiality. This is done not only through words or explanation but also through methods, and the point of methods is to gain experience.

So, the principle of the Dzogchen teachings is to discover our real nature, our potentiality, but not just in the sense of believing something. The principle is *not* believing. We can believe something is true today, then discover that it is false tomorrow. What we need is to discover our real nature through our experiences. For example, if I have never tasted chocolate and someone explains to me what chocolate tastes like, I can imagine it but I can never really be sure because I don't have first-hand knowledge. But if I taste a small piece of chocolate, that is unforgettable because it is my own experience.

In terms of everyday experience, in the Dzogchen teachings we talk of 'being aware' in daily life under any circumstances. In the Mahayana Buddhist system, being aware means observing our thoughts. If they are negative, then we transform them into positive thoughts and make sure we have good intentions. From the Dzogchen point of view, it is slightly different. In Dzogchen there is no rule. We cannot say whether something is good or bad, for this depends on the circumstances. Something might be good for me but bad for another person. In the Dzogchen teachings, therefore, we talk of 'being aware', which means we work with our circumstances: we see how they manifest and then we do our best. It is not always easy to understand a situation and know the best way to act, but we always try to do our best. And by doing practice, we develop more clarity.

All Tibetan traditions speak a lot about their point of view or way of seeing. Frequently there are conflicts between different schools of thought, with each school wishing to protect its own point of view. In the Dzogchen teachings, however, we don't consider the way of seeing, *tawa*, in the same manner. *Tawa* is not something we use to look outside ourselves and judge others. In the Dzogchen teachings, we use the example of glasses and the mirror. Glasses are used to look at outer things so we can judge and analyse them. But in Dzogchen we use a mirror, not glasses. If you look in a mirror, you see your face. Of course you cannot see your limitations and problems, but you can see your face. Generally, whenever there is a problem, we look outside ourselves for the cause. We are always ready to accuse other people and see their faults, but we never look at ourselves. Using the mirror means that we *are* looking at ourselves. We are discovering our own condition and our limitations, how we really are.

In the Dzogchen teachings we say that the most important thing is discovering our real nature of mind. But first we must discover our own everyday mind. If we never discover in a real sense our own mind and its limitations, then we are jumping too quickly into the real nature of the mind. It does not make any sense. So it is very, very important that first we actually understand our real condition and also our relative condition: our physical body, our energy and our mind, and how these relate to our existence and our own world with all its problems.

In the Dzogchen teachings, we understand everything to be related to its cause. If we have a stomach problem, maybe we have eaten something which does not suit us. When we discover the cause, then there is the possibility of overcoming our problem. So, for example, if you feel lazy and you don't feel like doing any Dzogchen practice, there is a reason for it and it is much better to discover the cause and work with it than to struggle with it. This is particularly true of Dzogchen practice, because if you are all wound up and tense and force yourself to practise without being relaxed, then you can never get into your real nature. That is why in Dzogchen we never force anything. Even if we occasionally feel lazy, we don't force anything but try to remain aware of what is happening. That is the main point. If we are not distracted and give ourselves space, then we can discover the cause of our problems. In this way, we needn't *have* any problems. This is one of the most important principles of the Dzogchen teachings.

Being aware means having a certain presence. But how can we learn to have a continuation of this presence? This can happen in different ways through learning contemplation. In the Dzogchen teachings, we use the term 'contemplation' rather than 'meditation'. Meditation generally means to meditate on something, which is a kind of concept. With contemplation, there is no concept to focus on, no form or colour. We just remain in our real nature. In the teachings, if someone is a really good practitioner of Dzogchen, then there is a continuation of presence. Contemplation is also related to the transmission of the teachings. Through following a teacher and receiving instructions we can have experiences, and through these experiences we discover what it means to be in a state of contemplation.

When we are present, this means that we are not distracted. We always try to be aware, whatever the situation. For example, if we go into the kitchen to make a cup of tea, we can make a kind of commitment: 'I want to be aware until I have succeeded in making this cup of tea.' And then we get up, walk into the kitchen, prepare the tea and take it out of the kitchen. And we may succeed in doing all this with presence or we may be distracted by lots of thoughts.

Driving a car is one way in which we can have a very precise experience of presence. Anybody who drives has to have presence. Even when you look to the right or left or you are talking, you still have to be present, otherwise you will have an accident. We can learn presence driving a car, but we can also learn it in daily life. For example, if you are distracted when you are cooking, instead of cutting the vegetables or meat, you will cut your finger. So this kind of presence is very, very useful in daily life, and in the Dzogchen teachings, it is a kind of practice. But this is not contemplation. This gives you some idea of what the Dzogchen view means.

On the Dzogchen path, another important point is practice, or application of the teachings, which you should learn from your teacher. Our attitude and conduct are also very important. I have already told you that the most important thing is to be aware and not distracted. These are the three main points of the path.

Dzogchen, then, means our real nature or potentiality, but to discover our real nature we have the Dzogchen teachings. The teachings help us discover our real nature. Once you have an understanding of Dzogchen, then you can also understand different Buddhist teachings, such as Sutra or Tantra. There are many different methods, but the aim of them all is for individuals to discover their real nature and remain in it. This is very, very important. The teachings exist for the individual and not the individual for the teachings. This is the Dzogchen way of seeing. In Dzogchen, all the different teachings exist for the individual to realize their true nature and to develop that knowledge. If you use the teachings like this, they will be more beneficial to you and you will not become confused. It is easy to become limited by a teaching, but the point of the teachings is *not* to limit ourselves. Some teachers also teach in a limited way, but you must understand that this is not really correct. The teachings are a means to wake you up, open your eyes and make you understand that you have many limitations.

Limitations are the manifestation of dualistic vision, and

dualistic vision is the source of suffering, of *samsara*. So we follow the teachings in order to become free of our limitations and gain liberation. This is how the teachings must work. Many people think that if they follow a teaching and then change to another tradition, this will lead to conflict. This should not be the case because the teachers themselves must be realized, enlightened, which means they must have gone beyond limitations. No one can be realized and remain limited at the same time.

It is through the teachings of the Buddha, *dharma*, that we discover the meaning of all phenomena, including ourselves and our real condition. That is the real meaning of the teachings of *dharma*. But if we don't understand or use *dharma* correctly, then instead of being a cause of liberation, it can also be a force for cyclic existence, or *samsara*. A very famous teacher, Atisha, said, 'If you are not using *dharma*, what is *dharma*? *Dharma* can also be the cause of *samsara*.' This is very true. If we pretend to be practising *dharma* at the same time as being involved in worldly things with our own self-interest and limitations, we create many problems for ourselves. We already have infinite limitations, which is why we are in *samsara*. We don't need to develop any more limitations, but to discover our limitations and free ourselves from them.

Look at yourself in the mirror and then you can really dis-cover yourself, become free and enter into the teachings in a real sense. In this way, *dharma* can be beneficial for all sentient beings, not only people who are considered spiritual but even people who are not seriously interested in the teachings. *Dharma* is useful for everybody.

CHÖGYAL NAMKHAI NORBU

ACKNOWLEDGEMENTS

First and foremost we would like to thank Chögyal Namkhai Norbu for his great generosity and support throughout this project, especially for answering our endless questions and for giving permission to use extracts from his London talk, 1994, as a foreword. Without his blessing, this book would never have been written. We would also like to express our deep appreciation to both his Tibetan translators, Adriano Clemente and Jim Valby, for their meticulous checking of the manuscript at various stages of the work and for their astute suggestions.

We would also like to thank the following: Tsultrim Allione, Dr Gyurme Dorje and Robert Beer, who kindly read the manuscript and offered their valuable views and comments. Fabbio Andrico, Geoffrey Blundell, Cara Denman, Catriona Mundle, Marianne Sheehan, Richard Steven and Dorothee von Greiff also read the manuscript in the early stages and made helpful suggestions. Chloë Abbatt, Stephen Batchelor, Dr Martin Boord, Mike Dickman, Mike Farmer, Mike Gilmore, Dominic Kennedy, Andy Lukianowicz, Ossian MacLise (Sangye Nyenpa) and Richard Williamson all brought their particular areas of Tibetan expertise to the text, which was invaluable. In addition, useful contributions were made by Des Barry, Nigel Hamilton, Lama

Tenpai Nyima, Dr Rupert Sheldrake, Swami Atmachaitanya and Stoffelina Verdonk. Finally, thanks are also due to Richard Austin, the Allan family, Thomas Beaver, Dolma Beresford, Luke Beresford, Marie Beresford, Susan Burrows, Julia, Tristram and George Hull, Natasha Lawless, Hetty MacLise, John Shane, Kasha and Maciek Sikora, Sogyal Rinpoche and Stephen Turoff for their encouragement and support ... and to Rusky for her patience. At HarperCollins, we would especially like to acknowledge and thank Carole Tonkinson, our commissioning editor, as well as Kate Latham, Simon Gerratt, Jacqueline Burns, Kathryn Whinney, Jacqui Caulton and Lizzie Hutchins for her sensitive editing.

Without the inspiration and guidance of the dakinis, this project would never have reached fruition. We take full responsibility for any errors and omissions contained in the text, which do not reflect in any way upon the peerless lineage of Dzogchen masters or the Dzogchen teachings. This book was finished on the Full Moon of March 2003, the anniversary of the great Dzogchen master Garab Dorje.

CHAPTER 1

DZOGCHEN:
THE GREAT PERFECTION

'The Dzogchen teachings are neither a philosophy, nor a religious doctrine, nor a cultural tradition. Understanding the message of the teachings means discovering one's own true condition stripped of all the self-deceptions and falsifications which the mind creates. The very meaning of the Tibetan term Dzogchen, "Great Perfection", refers to the true primordial state of every individual and not to any transcendent reality.' [1]

Dzogchen, which means 'Great Perfection', is a spiritual tradition found both within Tibetan Buddhism and the ancient Bon, or pre-Buddhist, heritage of Tibet. Within the Tibetan Buddhist framework, the teachings of Dzogchen, which are also known as *Atiyoga*, meaning 'Primordial Yoga', are seen as the culmination or pinnacle of all the Buddhist paths of realization. In essence, the Dzogchen tradition is an inner or heart teaching which is complete in itself, having its own distinct practices and lineage. As an esoteric path, it is characterized by its direct and unelaborate approach, for it is fundamentally free of dependence on any outer forms or rituals. However, the term *Dzogchen* can also be used to mean the 'self-perfected' state of mind of the individual, the non-dual state beyond words or description.

The Dzogchen teachings are principally concerned with show-ing the way in which we all, as individuals, can take responsibility for our own situation, rather than looking outside ourselves for a solution, whether this to another person, a state, an institution or a belief system.

Even though the term 'Dzogchen tradition' is frequently employed, this fundamentally does not refer to a system of belief or a type of philosophy which can be 'adopted'. Once we start thinking that there is something specific to 'accept' or 'reject', we are entering into the dualistic process of 'possessor' and 'possessed', of subject and object. Knowledge of Dzogchen is therefore not something which we can 'take on' if we choose, but rather some-thing we discover, like taking off a mask to unveil our true face.

'Dzogchen is not a school or sect, or a religious system. It is simply a state of knowledge which masters have transmitted beyond any limits of sect or monastic tradition. In the lineage of the Dzogchen teachings there have been masters belonging to all social classes, including farmers, nomads, nobles, monks and great religious fig-ures, from every spiritual tradition or sect.'[2]

Throughout history, Dzogchen masters and practitioners have in fact defied allegiance to any particular religion, sect, social rank or institutional structure, and have lived in the most diverse of situations. There have been famous Dzogchen teachers of great public stature, such as the fifth Dalai Lama of Tibet, as well as humble monks and lay practitioners, both men and women. Today, Dzogchen masters and practitioners can be found within all the schools of traditional Tibetan Buddhism – Nyingma, Kagyu, Sakya and Gelugpa[fn1] – as well as within the ancient Bon tradition. The present Dalai Lama, for example, is a Dzogchen master and a Gelugpa monk as well as being the political and spiritual leader of Tibet. The late Nyingma teachers H.H. Dudjom Rinpoche and H.H. Dilgo Khyentse were great Dzogchen masters who also taught extensively in the West.

'The Great Perfection teachings have been around for thousands of years. It is not something that the Tibetans invented ... the Dzogchen masters brought it from India, but even before that it was around ... for thirteen hundred years the Tibetans have made great efforts to preserve and uphold these sublime and profound teachings. Suddenly, they are being offered to the whole world, for the benefit of all. This the moment of Dzogchen!'[3]

Worldwide interest in the Dzogchen tradition has increased enormously over the last few years and the teachings are now more widespread and accessible in the West than they have ever been, even in Tibet.

Amongst the foremost contemporary Tibetan teachers of this ancient tradition is the master Chögyal Namkhai Norbu. In the mid-70s he began to teach a few Western students, first in Italy and soon afterwards in other European countries and America. Since then, he has continued to explain and transmit the Dzogchen teachings with tireless dedication to thousands of students all over the world, since Dzogchen's quintessential and non-dogmatic approach resonates among people of all cultures and nationalities.

'Many people today are not interested in spiritual matters, and their lack of interest is reinforced by the generally materialistic outlook of our society. If you ask them what they believe in, they may even say that they don't believe in anything. Such people think that all religion is based on faith, which they regard as little better than superstition, with no relevance to the modern world. But Dzogchen cannot be regarded as a religion, and does not ask anyone to

3

believe in anything. Rather, it suggests that the individual observe him or herself, and discover what his or her actual condition is.'[4]

Other contemporary Dzogchen teachers include Sogyal Rinpoche, a Nyingma lama who is well known for his understanding of Western culture and particularly for his insightful work into death and dying, Thinley Norbu, the son of H.H. Dudjom Rinpoche, Lama Tharchin and a number of younger Nyingmapa lamas. The late Nyoshul Khenpo was both a Dzogchen meditation master and poet who wrote eloquently about Dzogchen. Another great Dzogchen master, recently deceased, Tulku Urgyen Rinpoche, comments, 'Even the word *Dzogchen* is world renowned.'[5]

A teaching which is not dependent on externals can obviously be transposed from one culture to another more readily than one which places greater emphasis on outer forms and requires some manner of conformity.

'… Dzogchen does not depend on externals; rather it is a teaching about the essentials of the human condition … since the Dzogchen teachings are not dependent on culture, they can be taught, under-stood and practised in any cultural context.'[6]

It is because of its quintessential nature that the practice of Dzogchen lends itself more readily to the Western lifestyle than some other types of discipline, which are more dependent on outer structures or rituals. To be a practitioner of Dzogchen, one does not need to change anything externally – one's clothes, one's job or one's way of life.

'… when you practise the teachings of Dzogchen you must understand your capacity and your culture. Everyone has their understanding connected to their attitude and their culture. You can

use this and through your culture you can enter into understanding and develop ... you must not confuse the culture with the teaching ... You must not change your culture. There is nothing to throw away.' [7]

In the Dzogchen tradition, it is said that a practitioner should always try to integrate or adapt themselves totally to the situation and conditions in which they find themselves. In general, this means that an individual should be fully aware of the society and circumstances in which they live and respect its conventions and customs. However, this does not mean to say that they should be conditioned or attached to such customs. A good practitioner is considered to be someone who has integrated the state of contemplation within themselves in such a complete way that whatever their circumstances may be, there need be no outward indication that they are practising at all!

Historically speaking, it is partly because there is nothing to show or change externally that the practice of Dzogchen has often been considered a 'hidden' path.

THE HIDDEN PATH

Dzogchen is often spoken about as a secret or hidden path because of its lack of external show. Also, as Chögyal Namkhai Norbu explains, when it first arrived in India, it threatened the stability of the existing religious institutions by challenging individuals to break free of their spiritual conditioning:

'When the teaching of Dzogchen arrived in India from Oddiyana [fn2] *[our present-day Swat Valley region of Pakistan], both as transmission and as an object of study, many teachers of Dzogchen performed their transmissions and practices at midnight, or hidden in caves*

*where no one could find them. Many people have said as a result that
Dzogchen is secret. But this isn't true. The reason they were secretive
and hidden is that had they been open, the king and various Indian
authorities would have put them in jail. In that epoch in India, Sutric
Buddhism was widespread, with many monastic institutions ... and
... Dzogchen was perceived as something dangerous because the
teaching of Dzogchen has nothing to do with institutions ...*

*When we talk about the Dzogchen teachings, the principal thing
being communicated, taught and learnt is "awareness" and the
way of bringing this awareness into one's immediate present existence. This replaces everything which is normally represented by
and performed by institutions. There is no institution or structure
which corresponds to all people and all needs, so in truth, institutions mean conditioning people. The Dzogchen teachings make one
discover this, not only about institutions, but [also about] oneself
and one's conditioning of any kind ...'*[8]

Thus the path of Dzogchen was considered secret from the outset not only because it threatened existing institutions but also
because the very premise on which it was based could be seen
as revolutionary by more traditional or hierarchical systems of
knowledge. Dzogchen is founded on the fundamental understanding that all beings are self-perfected, i.e. already enlightened, and that this knowledge simply needs to be reawakened.
Essentially, there is nothing to strive for or attain.

'*The essence is within yourself and you must not be conditioned
by externals, by a book or a system ... Dzogchen practitioners must
be aware and free and able to use everything, control everything,
without being conditioned by the teachings or by externals.*'[9]

Later, the Dzogchen teachings were considered to be secret

because of their profundity and in Tibet were generally only transmitted to those considered to have sufficient capacity or depth of understanding. It was even said, particularly within the monasteries, that Dzogchen was only for realized beings and not for ordinary people at all. But this view cannot be correct, because if a person is already realized, then they have no need of any teachings, Dzogchen or otherwise!

'Many people think that Dzogchen is something very mysterious or secret ... sometimes it seems as if you just can't talk about it. Sometimes when we speak of Dzogchen, people are amazed and say: "How can you speak to the public like that about Dzogchen? You have to know what the consequences are ... it's a secret thing."

I'm not in the least bit worried about this. If somebody establishes a bad relationship with the Dzogchen teachings, it's many thousands of times better than having no relationship at all. Of course, if you have a good relationship to the Dzogchen teachings, that's even better, and many people may even understand something. In this sense, I don't see the sense of the secretiveness.'[10]

But this doesn't mean to say that all people are identical and are automatically suited to the practice of Dzogchen. Indeed, Dzogchen is also called 'self-secret', because if those who do not have the appropriate karma for understanding hear or reflect on the teachings, they will not penetrate their meaning. They transcend the judgement of the ordinary mind. However, it is not a question of being better or worse, rather a question of appropriateness. The very intimation that Dzogchen is the right path for everyone, or indeed that Buddhism is the right religion for everyone, is inimical to the very essence of the Buddha's teachings, which emphasize individual responsibility and freedom.

Tulku Urgyen Rinpoche describes Dzogchen as being sealed

with three types of secrecy: primordial secrecy (self-secret), hidden secrecy (the teachings are not evident to everyone) and concealed secrecy (kept deliberately secret). Some specific Dzogchen practice methods are not spoken about openly to protect the integrity of the transmission.

But there is still another interpretation of why Dzogchen is often termed a hidden teaching. There are many tales of great Dzogchen practitioners whose practice was invisible outwardly yet who attained a high level of realization. They lived their whole lives without anyone recognizing they were following a spiritual path at all because it was impossible to see any outer signs of their inner commitment. Indeed, sometimes, because their practice was completely hidden or internalized, their true spiritual qualities were only recognized at their death.

STORIES OF DZOGCHEN PRACTITIONERS

There are many stories of renowned Dzogchen practitioners who lived completely incognito, preferring to avoid all the pomp and ceremony of more ritualistic approaches to religion. Chögyal Namkhai Norbu's own principal Dzogchen teacher Changchub Dorje was of such an unassuming disposition. In terms of outward appearance he seemed like a normal country person of Tibet. He also served as the village doctor, often attending to many sick people each day. Around him, his disciples also lived in a very ordinary way, most of them being very simple people, not at all well-to-do, who grew and tended crops, working on the land and practising together. In Chögyal Namkhai Norbu's own words:

'... if I were to see my master Changchub Dorje now, no one seeing him amongst you could know that he was a great practitioner or *great master. There are many, many practitioners of Dzogchen who are like that. You can't observe anything outwardly about them. So it is not said that a person of great spirit or of elevated spirituality must necessarily present himself in silken robes or anything of that kind. It's very difficult to judge that which just shows itself from the outside.'* [11]

Another young Tibetan lama, Tanpei Nyima, described his own contemporary Dzogchen teacher, Tenzin Wang-gyal, in a similar fashion:

'He was very respected throughout the region [of Amdo in eastern Tibet] and so many people came to ask for his help and to request teachings. They would usually make some kind of offering to him in exchange, so I know he had plenty of money. Yet even if a well-known lama came to visit him he didn't put on any special type of clothes or robes to receive him – because he didn't have any! He was always dressed in the same simple garments, which even got quite dirty and yet it didn't seem to bother him at all. It was the same with his meals. He could have afforded really expensive food, yet he would eat very simple things. Sometimes I would prepare his meal, but if I asked him if he would like this or that to eat he would always answer "It doesn't matter." People in general were a little afraid or nervous of him because although he was always very kind to everyone, he didn't speak very much, and he had a certain quality or presence about him.' [12]

One of the greatest Dzogchen masters of the nineteenth century was Patrul Rinpoche. Although he was a popular teacher, poet and author, and revered as a great lama, he often travelled anonymously throughout eastern Tibet, dressed in a nomad's tattered full-length sheepskin coat. One account tells of how he went unrecognized even by a group of fellow lamas:

'Once Patrul Rinpoche came upon a band of lamas who were on their way to a great gathering, and he joined their party. He was so raggedly outfitted, so self-effacing, that he was treated as an ordinary mendicant practitioner. He had to help make the tea, gather firewood, and serve the monks of the party while they travelled through a remote region of Kham in eastern Tibet.'[13]

Eventually, during the course of the ceremonial gathering, while taking an initiation from another great lama who had the clarity of mind to see beyond mere appearances, he was finally recognized as none other than the living Buddha, the supreme Dzogchen master Dza Patrul. Then, while the assembled masses gaped, the grand presiding master stepped down from his throne and prostrated himself again and again before the ragged vagabond.

As a practitioner of Dzogchen, Patrul Rinpoche was always keen to escape from any formal occasion. Even when he was asked to give a teaching, he would do his best to explain something for one or two days, then he would just slip away and no one would see him for months!

In another delightful story, he found himself in the position of receiving his own teachings from a humble monk:

'One day Patrul Rinpoche was in the mountains and came upon a cave. There was a monk there in retreat and Patrul asked if he could have some teachings. The monk, who was a modest and true practitioner and not knowing that this was Patrul Rinpoche, said, "Honestly, I don't know much; I don't know what to teach you." But Patrul Rinpoche replied, "Whatever you practise, you can give me that teaching." "But," the monk said, "all I know is a little of the preparatory teaching that Patrul Rinpoche has written ..." Patrul said, "Fine! Teach me a little of that." So the monk agreed ...

Eventually, some disciples of Patrul Rinpoche discovered their *master was going up into the mountains every day to the cave and went to ask the monk, "Is it true that Patrul Rinpoche comes to you every day?" "Patrul Rinpoche!" he exclaimed. "Don't be silly. Some old man comes up here and has asked me to teach him so I am teaching him the preparatory Ngöndro of Patrul Rinpoche." They said, "You're crazy. That is Patrul Rinpoche ..."*

The next day when Patrul came up the mountain as he always did, the monk had closed his cave and refused to open it ... so Patrul Rinpoche said, "Here I am, doing my practice calmly with this monk and some devils have disturbed me." After that, many people came to ask him for teachings. He stayed for two or three days to please them, then he escaped. This was not only true of Patrul Rinpoche, but of many of the teachers of Dzogchen ... many of them were not very well cultivated or well-organized intellectual [types].' [14]

Not only did Dzogchen practitioners often present themselves in this very humble way, but some also made a point of actively ridiculing more formal or systematic approaches to religion through their 'crazy wisdom', like the great Tantric yogis or Mahasiddhas of India. The wandering yogi Drukpa Kunley, a Tibetan master of Tantra and Dzogchen, was famous for his outrageous acts and spontaneous songs:

> *'In this Religious Centre of Holy Lhasa*
> *Incense and butter lamps are the customary offerings*
> *To our Only Mother, the Glorious Goddess;*
> *But today, Duty-Free Kunga Legpa*
> *Offers his penis and his turquoise.*
> *Accept it, Goddess, and show us compassion!'* [15]

Most people thought that Drukpa Kunley was utterly mad, yet for him all sensory forms were the path! In fact, he used his 'madness' to cut through customary forms of behaviour as a means of pointing out the limitations in conventional ways of thinking.

What becomes clear from such stories is that real spiritual depth has nothing to do with outward appearances, fame, titles, intellectual or academic knowledge or even performing conventional kindly actions, but more to do with having direct experience of the true nature of one's own mind. This state, which is beyond words, is known in the Dzogchen tradition as 'the primordial state', and direct knowledge of it is called *rigpa*.

'Dzog means "perfect" and chen means "great". So Dzogchen means the "Great Perfection" ... the primordial state of consciousness of the individual is the Great Perfection. When you live in this knowledge, in this state, then that is practice. Dzogchen is not outside you ... it is the Great Perfection of the original or primordial state of consciousness.'[16]

The emphasis in Dzogchen is on finding this experience for oneself through various methods; thus it is called 'the direct path' as opposed to 'the gradual path'. In the context of Tibetan Buddhism, Dzogchen is the path of self-liberation.

FOOTNOTES

[fn1] Nyingmapa (*rnying ma pa*): The oldest tradition of Tibetan Buddhism based on the teachings of Padmasambhava.

Kagyudpa (*bka' brgyud pa*): An early partially reformed order based on the monastic system of the Kadampa combined with Tantric practices of the yogins and lay practitioners.

Sakyapa (*sa skya pa*): One of the four major sects of Tibetan Buddhism, stressing both intellectual learning and meditation.

Gelugpa (*dge lugs pa*): The reformed sect of Tibetan Buddhist, founded by Tsongkapa in the fourteenth century.

[fn2] Oddiyana is considered the land where both Tantric and Dzogchen teachings originated.

CHAPTER 2

THE BUDDHA'S TEACHINGS

'The experience is as natural as sun and moon light;
Yet it is beyond both space and time.
It is beyond all words and description ...'[1]

Shakyamuni Buddha is revered as the source of the Buddhist teachings, or *dharma*, and is considered one of 12 ancient primordial masters of Dzogchen. Born as an Indian prince in 563 BC, he turned away from the affluent life dictated by his royal birth after seeing the effects of pain, old age and death beyond the palace walls and became a wandering mendicant until he attained enlightenment. He taught the way to overcome the inherent suffering of cyclic existence and the basis of his teachings was the Four Noble Truths.

Having understood the inevitability of worldly suffering, the first noble truth of the Buddhist path, the Buddha advised that rather than fight or struggle against it we should seek directly for its origin, because it is only by understanding the cause that it is possible to deal with the problem at its source. The second noble truth which the Buddha subsequently taught is concerned with identifying the cause of suffering. Knowing that cause and effect are interrelated, he discovered that the only way to overcome suffering at its root is go beyond our habitual dualistic perception. That is the third noble truth of the Buddhist path. The fourth and final noble truth that the Buddha taught refers to actually setting out on the path that leads to the cessation of suffering – the path that led to his own enlightenment.

> 'As a flame blown out by the wind
> Goes to rest and cannot be defined,
> So the wise man freed from individuality
> Goes to rest and cannot be defined.
> Gone beyond all images
> Gone beyond the power of words.'[2]

When the Buddha tried to communicate his experience of realization, or enlightenment, to others directly, he said it was 'beyond words'. Speechless, he simply held up a flower as a gesture of the truth. He had understood that complete release from suffering could only be achieved by overcoming all dualistic thinking at its source, that is, by returning to the primal condition beyond any separation of 'outer' and 'inner', between 'I' and 'other'. This 'primordial state' was not something that could be communicated using words, for it could only be understood through direct personal experience.

Although Buddhist theory presents a complex philosophical framework and a sophisticated intellectual analysis of the mind abounding in explanations of this 'wordless' state, in the end a purely intellectual approach to the *angst* of being human is, at best, only provisional! Ultimately, the essence of all Buddhist teaching is aimed at reawakening within each individual an understanding of their own 'Buddha nature' through the practice and experience of meditation.

'It is quite impossible to find the Buddha anywhere other than in one's own mind.

A person who is ignorant of this may seek externally, but how is it possible to find oneself through seeking anywhere other than in oneself?' [3]

THREE PATHS

There are three distinct approaches to the understanding and practice of meditation within Tibetan Buddhism, known as Sutra, Tantra and Dzogchen. These different paths exist because there are countless individuals with different temperaments and abilities, so there is a method which is best suited to each person. Although the methods are different in each case, and although some take a more gradual and others a more direct, or non-gradual, route, the common goal is always that of overcoming dualistic perception by discovering the state which the Buddha described as being 'beyond words'.

If we examine our nature closely it becomes clear that we all have three main aspects or functions: our mind, with its mental activity, our energy (or voice), with its emotional activity, and our body, with its physical activity. In Buddhism, these are called the three 'doors' of body, voice and mind:

'Body includes the whole material dimension of the individual, while the voice is the vital energy of the body, known as prana *in Sanskrit and* lung *in Tibetan, the circulation of which is linked to the breathing. Mind includes both the mind that reasons and the nature of the mind, which is not subject to the limits of the intellect. The body, voice and mind of an ordinary being have become so conditioned that he or she has become completely caught up in dualism.'* [4]

The relationship between these three aspects can be compared to that of a rider on a horse. The mind is the rider, who needs to control the horse (the energy) in order to govern its direction (the physical body). However, although the mind is in the governing position, the physical body can also influence the energy, which can in turn influence the mind, thus all three aspects are interrelated and interdependent.

All the problems which we experience in our everyday lives are linked to one of these three aspects and when we perform any kind of Buddhist practice it generally concentrates on one or more of these three 'doors'. In general, the Sutra teachings are said to be linked with the body and controlling the physical dimension of our existence. Tantric practice, by contrast, is more related with our energy, by working with the emotions and controlling the breath. The Dzogchen teachings approach the level of the mind directly and in this sense Dzogchen could be said to be the most subtle as well as the most direct of these three paths. To understand Dzogchen in context, however, we need to examine first the paths of Sutra and Tantra.

SUTRA: THE PATH OF RENUNCIATION

The Sutra teachings are based on a collection of texts which directly relate the words taught by Shakyamuni Buddha to his human disciples.

One of the first concepts explained in the Sutra texts is the law of *karma*, or the law of cause and effect, which includes the notion of reincarnation. According to the law of *karma*, our present life experience is conditioned by our former actions and lives, while our future experiences and lives are governed inevitably by our present actions. Attaining a human birth is consequently considered a precious opportunity, since there is no guarantee that one will be reborn again as a human being. An individual is propelled on a ceaseless series of rebirths until they eventually find freedom from the wheel of existence through discovering the state of enlightenment or realization. Sutra practice is thus founded on the principle of accumulating merit through performing good actions and avoiding negative actions, so as to increase beneficial circumstances in the future.

In general, the Sutra teachings are known as the path of renunciation because an individual following this method may be obliged to give up a whole variety of things, such as sex and alcohol, and to avoid performing negative deeds. The Buddha observed that we experience many problems as a result of our passions or emotions, so in the Sutra system these are considered 'poisons' and an individual agrees to follow a strict code of rules to prevent themselves from being contaminated by these 'poisons'. This is the code of the Vinaya followed by monks, nuns and other practitioners following basic Sutra teachings. The idea is that by avoiding or eliminating the factors in our lives which inflame our feelings or fuel our emotions, we don't experience the same kind of problems. It is as simple as that!

The Sutric path is divided into Hinayana and Mahayana. In Hinayana, a practitioner's behaviour is governed by vows of renunciation and moral discipline, while a Mahayana practitioner's behaviour is governed by the intention to benefit all beings. At the Mahayana level, the training is linked with generating good intention. An individual following the Mahayana path who commits themselves to acting always for the benefit of others is called a Bodhisattva[fn1], and the development of supreme compassion, or *bodhicitta*[fn2], is central to their practice.

Impermanence, that is, the transience of all phenomena, including human life, is fundamental to all Buddhist approaches, as exemplified by these words of the Buddha:

> 'The three worlds are impermanent as clouds in
>   autumn.
> The birth and death of beings are like a show.
> Human life lasts as long as a lightning flash
> And passes as swiftly as a cascade down a steep
>   mountain.'[5]

Moreover, the whole of life is itself no more than a dream or a magical illusion: it has no inherent substance. The inherent emptiness of all phenomena, a realization which arises through meditation and close observation of the nature of external objects and of the mind itself, also gives rise to the principle of 'interdependence'. In other words, all phenomena only exist in relationship to each other, rather than as independent entities.

In the Sutras, great emphasis is given to the understanding of emptiness, or *shunyata*, as being the ground of all existence. But this so-called 'emptiness' should not be understood as something nihilistic, because implicit in this idea is the promise of infinite potentiality, like a universal womb which can give birth to myriad things.

> 'Regarding mind:
> Mind does not exist,
> Its expression is luminosity.'[6]

Knowledge of 'emptiness', acquired both through intellectual reasoning and meditation, eventually gives birth to the primordial wisdom of *prajna paramita*, for which 'there can be no explanation, because it cannot be defined or limited by words, because it is not capable of being measured by the mind'.[7]

In the Mahayana teachings, the main methods used to progress on the path are the accumulation of merit (by performing good actions) on the one hand and the accumulation of wisdom (through meditation practice) on the other. This assumes that the practitioner proceeds along the path in a progressive manner, i.e. in a gradual way.

In fact, the Sutra path actually embraces both 'gradual' and 'non-gradual' approaches. The best known non-gradual Sutra approach in the West is Japanese Zen, which was introduced into America and Britain in the nineteenth century. Both Zen and Chinese Ch'an (from which it derives) accept the notion of an instantaneous or a direct experience of enlightenment, known as *satori*, and although outside the Tibetan Buddhist framework, they are both frequently compared with non-gradual Tibetan approaches such as Dzogchen. As the renowned Ch'an master Niu-t'ou Fa-Jung (AD 595–657) said:

> '*The highest principle cannot be explained:*
> *It is neither free nor bound.*
> *Lively and attuned to everything*
> *It is always right before you.*'[8]

However, to say that all these non-gradual or direct approaches are the same is an oversimplification. Zen and Ch'an are Sutra-based Mahayana traditions which emphasize the wisdom aspect of the path (as opposed to gaining merit), and thus focus on the realization of emptiness as exemplified by the *prajna paramita*. Moreover, neither Zen nor Ch'an have the same way of working with the emotions in the manner of Tantra or through the potentiality of energy as in Dzogchen. Thus, each of these three

approaches, apart from utilizing different methods, also expresses
or manifests the culmination of their realization in slightly different ways.

TANTRA: THE PATH OF TRANSFORMATION

Unlike the Sutra teachings, the Tantric texts, or Tantras, were
not transmitted by the Buddha in his human form directly, nor
were they written down by other teachers or scholars in an academic manner. All Tantric texts originate from the Buddha, or
other masters, via a manifestation through light in a visionary
dimension.

Although Shakyamuni Buddha taught Tantric teachings to
beings in another dimension, he predicted that he would manifest in the future to propagate these teachings in this dimension
and prophesied that he would be reborn in a lake. According
to legend, the second Buddha, Padmasambhava, was born in
Oddiyana, present-day Pakistan, in the eighth century, from a
lotus in a lake and travelled to Tibet in AD 747. He is a principal
source of Tibetan Tantric teachings and one of the chief lineage-
holders of the Dzogchen tradition.

The term *Tantra* literally means 'continuity', referring to the
ceaseless flow of energy within the individual. It is this energy,
derived from the emotions, which is the central aspect of
Tantric practice.

*'In tantra, the principle isn't that one has to construct something to
obtain realization, but that one is realised as one is, from the start
… and that one does not transform this self-perfected state or condition, but the relative aspect … So transformation means that all
our vision is transformed into pure vision and this simultaneously*

includes the concept of shunyata, *that is, void, otherwise there would be no possibility of transformation.'*[9]

The Tantric path assumes knowledge of emptiness or *shunyata* from the outset, otherwise how can the relative condition, that is our 'seemingly' material reality, be transformed into its purified aspect?

The actual means of bringing about this process of transformation can be gradual or non-gradual, according to the specific level of Tantric practice employed. For example, in certain Tantric practices such as Chakrasamvara or Hevajra, the visualization of the deity and its dimension, or *mandala*, which is the embodiment of one's own pure state, is gradually built up step by step, until it is complete. In other Tantric practices, such as Vajrakilaya or Sihamukha, the entire visualization is instantaneous.

The fuel which enables the Tantric transformation to take place is derived from the powerful charge contained within our emotions and passions. Unlike the Sutra approach, from the perspective of Tantra we recognize that our emotions have value, for they have a strong energy which is linked to our primordial potentiality. Our emotions are therefore something to be used in the practice, once they have been understood and transformed into their purified aspects. The dynamic between male and female energy is also fundamental to Tantra, where the male represents form or method and the female represents the energy or wisdom aspect of the primordial state.

'Tantra teaches not to suppress or destroy energy but to transmute it: in other words, go with the pattern of energy ... When you go with the pattern of energy, then experience becomes very creative ... You realize that you no longer have to abandon anything ... You begin to see the underlying qualities of wisdom in your life-situation.'[10]

The image of gold is used in the Tantric teachings to show how the same substance can be seen in a variety of different ways, even if its inherent nature always remains constant. For example, if a piece of gold is used to fashion the image of a Buddha or Bodhisattva and placed on a shrine, it becomes the object of worship, whereas if it is used to fashion a necklace, it is seen as a purely secular item. Our ideas of 'pure' and 'impure' are therefore very relative. In the same way, our emotions can be seen as something purely mundane or as something sacred to be used on the path.

The Tantric path is also called the Vajrayana, or 'diamond path', because it uses the *vajra*, the diamond thunderbolt, as a symbol of the individual. According to Chögyal Namkhai Norbu, the form of the *vajra* represents our own essential inner condition. The five points at one end stand for the five principal 'poisons' of anger, pride, attachment (desire), jealousy and ignorance. When we are governed by our emotions and distracted by them, we see everything in terms of impure vision. The five points at the other end of the *vajra* represent our five passions once they have been transformed into their purified aspect. In their real nature they become the five wisdoms: mirror-like wisdom, the wisdom of equality, discriminating wisdom, action-accomplishing wisdom and the wisdom of the fundamental condition of existence. The energy of the emotions is therefore valuable as each emotion has the inherent potential to be transformed into its respective quality of wisdom.

At the centre of the *vajra* is a small round ball, which represents our primordial potentiality, or our real nature, which is the state beyond limitation, the condition beyond the duality of the two extremes. In this state, an individual is no longer conditioned by their passions, because the real nature of things is beyond any kind of concept of pure or impure, good or bad, for it is beyond duality. In Tantric practice, this condition of non-duality is called Mahamudra and is synonymous with the state of Dzogchen. The only difference is in the methods used – the former is gradual and the latter non-gradual.

DZOGCHEN: THE PATH OF SELF-LIBERATION

'Dzogpa Chenpo is the path of luminous absorption,
the essence of the ultimate definitive meaning,
And the summit of the teachings of sutras and tantras:
This is the meaning of the instructions on the direct
approach
To the ultimate nature, the Buddha-essence as it is.' [11]

The Dzogchen teaching is not a path of renunciation or transformation, but rather the path of self-liberation. What does this mean? The main objective in the Dzogchen teachings is not to suppress or transform the emotions but to be able to find oneself directly in the 'real condition' or 'primordial state'. In Dzogchen, there are no specific rules to follow as in the Sutra tradition, neither are there specific commitments or promises to keep, as in the Tantric tradition. The only guideline to follow is one's own awareness. In this sense a great deal of responsibility is placed on the individual.

'Dzogchen has no rules. There is no law – but awareness … Only one vow exists: the intention to live in my own state, in my own primordial consciousness.' [12]

Since in Dzogchen the principal aim is to understand and enter into this state of knowledge directly, then it doesn't matter if outer things appear pure or impure, beautiful or ugly. The real point is not whether something is beautiful or ugly – what matters is our response to it, because it is only through our judgement of things and our subsequent feelings of attachment or aversion that we fall into the dualistic condition. The great Indian yogi Tilopa taught his disciple Naropa that: 'The problem is not pure or impure vision, but our own attachment.' [13] If one really understands this point then it is possible to 'liberate' any emotion.

Tantra uses antidotes to combat our main passions of ignorance, desire (attachment) and anger by transforming them into their peaceful, joyous and wrathful aspects, but in Dzogchen one does not need to change anything. Yet how can we experience pleasure, for example, without having attachment? It is by being in the state of 'instant presence', with awareness, and by self-liberating the attachment, rather than getting caught up in it or following the feelings or thoughts evoked by it. This is why Dzogchen is termed the path of self-liberation.

'There exists a natural, self-originated condition, the true and ultimate essence of the mind; if we leave it in its state of pure instantaneous presence, without seeking to modify it in any way, then its spontaneous and primordial wisdom will manifest nakedly.' [14]

FOOTNOTES

[fn1] *Bodhisattva* (Skt) (Tib. *byang chub sems dpa*): One who has taken the vow to guide all beings to enlightenment.

[fn2] *Bodhicitta* (Skt) (Tib. *byang chub sems*): Primordial mind.

CHAPTER 3

MIRROR OF THE MIND

'It is space, ungraspable as a thing.
It is a flawless precious clear crystal.
It is the lamp-like radiance of your own self-
  illuminated mind.
It is inexpressible, like the experience of a mute.
It is unobscured transparent wisdom.
The luminous Dharmakaya Buddha-nature.
Primordially pure and spontaneous.
It cannot be expressed in words.
In the space of Dharma
Forever overwhelming mind's inspection.'[1]

How does one attempt to express the inexpressible? How can this experience be communicated to others? In the Dzogchen teachings the symbol of the mirror is used a great deal as a way of illustrating the true nature of the mind. Rather than being involved in the reflections in the mirror and trying to change or modify them in any way, one enters into the condition of the mirror itself:

'We speak of the me-long [mirror] and of its purity, its limpidity and its qualification, which is its capacity to reflect that which is in

front of it. We cannot give up the reflections ... we must not ignore the reflections, that is, the relative [condition]. When you are not conditioned by the reflections, that means you have self-knowledge. But if you don't have self-knowledge, then you are living in the reflections. Then the reflections are good or bad, more or less important, beautiful or ugly – and all those distinctions.'[2]

Our primordial condition, or the essence of our mind and of the universe, is completely untainted or pure from the very beginning. It is like a polished mirror or an azure blue sky which is utterly limitless, empty and clear. Our thoughts, feelings and the whole of manifest existence are really like clouds which pass across the empty canvas of the sky when the wind blows them there, or reflections which flicker across the glass of a mirror when something passes before it. They are just illusory. Our real nature is empty yet full of infinite potentiality. It is beyond form or description.

'Just as the nature of the mirror cannot receive any harm or benefit from the appearance of a reflection, [so] liberation from existence occurs when one precisely discovers the state which is beyond mind.'[3]

There are therefore many ways of explaining our 'real nature' or 'primordial state' and there are a great variety of different methods and practices which can be utilized within Buddhism as a whole to discover this condition through first-hand experience. All the great Dzogchen masters have adapted their teachings according to the specific conditions and circumstances in which they have found themselves and to the individual capacity of their students. In Dzogchen, the master traditionally introduces a student directly to this non-dual state through a variety of different methods, using oral, symbolic or direct transmission.

The theory is explained using traditional texts and everyday language which accords with the situation, or is communicated through symbols, using images which include a crystal or a peacock's feather as well as a mirror. Yet it is only when the student has really recognized and experienced the state directly through a direct mind-to-mind transmission from a master or through the experience of practice that they can really begin to practise the Dzogchen teachings. Experience of the non-dual primordial state is the starting-point for the practice of Dzogchen, which is why this primordial condition is known as the 'base' in the Dzogchen tradition.

BASE, PATH AND FRUIT

The traditional way of introducing or explaining the fundamental principles of the Dzogchen teachings is in terms of the 'base', 'path' and 'fruit':

- The base refers to the primordial state which is the true inherent condition of the individual, which is pure from the very beginning.

- The path is the means and methods one uses to become more familiar with that knowledge – in other words, with the different forms of meditation practice which one uses to develop one's understanding and depth of experience.

- The fruit is the arrival point where all one's activities are completely integrated with the primordial state.

Base

'The base, or Zhi in Tibetan, is the term used to denote the fundamental ground of existence, both at the universal level and at the
level of the individual, the two being essentially the same; to realize
the one is to realize the other … It is called the base because it is the
base of all phenomena and because, being uncreated, ever pure
and self-perfected, it is not something that has to be constructed.'[4]

The base is divided into three aspects or divisions: 'essence',
'nature' and 'energy'. These should not be understood as distinct
qualities or attributes in themselves, for they co-exist simultaneously within ourselves as part of our base, or primordial state.
The image of the mirror is often used to symbolize these three
aspects or 'wisdoms':

❀ The 'essence' refers to the empty or void quality of the mind,
   which like a mirror, can reflect anything that appears in front
   of it, without discrimination. Since the essence of the mind is
   emptiness, this condition is synonymous with the calm state
   when the mind is quiescent and empty of thoughts.

❀ The 'nature' refers to a mirror's capacity to reflect objects with
   perfect accuracy and clarity, without being conditioned by
   them. The nature of the mind is clarity, which is synonymous
   with movement, as when a thought arises spontaneously.

❀ The 'energy' which acts through the uninterrupted continuity
   of the alternation of these two aspects, describes the way things
   manifest in the mirror. The reflections that arise in it are the
   energy of the mirror's own inherent nature manifesting visibly.

Likewise, the way things appear in our lives is simply the 'energy' of our mind's own nature manifesting externally.

The image here is like that of waves appearing on the smooth surface of the sea, rising and falling in an easy and uninterrupted fashion. The empty space between thoughts merges effortlessly into the movement of each thought as it arises and then subsides back into emptiness, all within the infinite ocean of our primordial state. In the Dzogchen view, the main principle is simply to be aware of what is presenting itself, without following thoughts or becoming attached to the empty condition:

'The essential principle is to ... maintain presence in the state of the moving wave of the thought itself ... If one considers the calm state as something positive to be attained, and the wave of thought as something negative to be abandoned, and one remains caught up in the duality of grasping and rejecting, there is no way of overcoming the ordinary state of mind.'[5]

Path

The path, or *lam* in Tibetan, refers to all the methods which are used to progress or develop this understanding. It is divided into three aspects: the 'view', 'practice' and 'conduct':

❋ The 'view' refers to self-observation, i.e. looking into the mirror of the mind as opposed to anything external to oneself. Most theoretical views or standpoints are concerned with making some kind of formulation about the world around us. In this case, however, the 'view' is nothing other than the examination of our own real condition.

❖ 'Practice' refers to the various meditation methods which are applied on the path to discover our real condition. The Dzogchen teachings are divided into three separate series of transmissions: the *Semde* (Mind Series), *Longde* (Space Series) and *Upadesha* (Essential Series). The emphasis within each series of teachings and the meditation methods used to attain the results of the practice vary within each section, yet each series is also complete within itself. The *Semde* series of practices, for example, contains many oral explanations aimed at introducing the state of contemplation and progressively developing one's experiences. The *Longde* series contains very little intellectual analysis and emphasizes being able to stabilize this understanding by making use of physical positions. The *Upadesha* series concentrates on methods to continue and develop this understanding.

❖ 'Conduct' or behaviour refers to the way of integrating both view and practice into our daily life.

Fruit

The fruit is the final goal or aim of the practice, a state of realization free from concept and beyond effort. Yet in truth the base, path and fruit in Dzogchen are indivisible, since all are related to the primordial condition. As Chögyal Namkhai Norbu says:

'... the path is not something strictly separate from the fruit, rather the process of self-liberation becomes ever deeper until the deluded consciousness that was unaware of the base which was always our own nature disappears: this is what is called the fruit.'[6]

Essentially, then, there is nothing to attain or achieve. We already possess our Buddha nature just as it is!

BUDDHA NATURE: AS IT IS

'The Dzogchen teaching serves to discover our own Dzogchen. So we are Dzogchen. This means that we are totally perfected, or, in other words, enlightened or realized from the very beginning.'[7]

The Three Kayas

Eventually, the mind becomes unified with the spacious, luminous, all-embracing quality of its own nature, the *dharmakaya*, the empty mind essence beyond limits or concept:

'Having no base, it is pure, lucid, expansive and empty from the very beginning. So whatever appears clear of its own volition is a quality of the expansive phenomena. Whatever concept or hope one has of this spacious nature, in reality the stable compassionate mind of dharmakaya *has descended from the beginning of time. It is self-empty, without change or variation.'*[8]

The *dharmakaya* is just one of the three *kayas*, or 'dimensions of being' (also known as the three bodies of the Buddha), which are the Tibetan terms used to represent the total perfection of an individual's body, voice and mind.

The state of enlightenment is thus described as having three aspects or levels of experience: *dharmakaya*, *sambogakaya* and *nirmanakaya*:

❖ The *dharmakaya* dimension is the pure, unborn nature of the mind in its ultimate emptiness and perfection.

❖ *Sambogakaya* means 'the dimension of complete enjoyment', the realm of pure vision suffused with richness and light which corresponds to the perfection of the voice or energy level.

❖ The *nirmanakaya* is the dimension of manifestation or emanation in which realized beings assume a physical form and act within the human plane: ultimate reality (divinity) as it appears in the bodily flesh.

'Whatever is perceived is the wisdom of the spontaneously occurring absolute nature, without action or effort, where this spacious joy spirals into one. Self-apparent clarity is inseparable from sambogakaya. *In whatever is perceived, this* sambogakaya *naturally and spontaneously exists. Modifying but never changing, simultaneously massive and encompassing.*

From the dance of all the distinctive characteristics of existence comes the self-arisen, astonishing nirmanakaya. *This is none other than the Buddha Samantabhadra.*[fn1] *This kind of compassion does not come from a particular place of prosperity: the compassionate mind itself being effortless and complete with the three* kayas. *It is not separate from the absolute nature, and not compounded but miraculously formed.'*[9]

All three aspects, however, are also inherent simultaneously within each individual in their own enlightened or realized state, although:

'Actually not even the term "realized" is really correct because it implies becoming something that we were not before. Total perfection

does not consist in realizing something, because realization is already perfect and always has been. Nor is talking about "enlightenment" actually correct because really there is nothing to enlighten. In fact, our state is like a lamp that does not need to be enlightened or illumined from outside: light, illumination, is its own nature. The state of Dzogchen is like light, there is nothing to enlighten.'[10]

Self-Liberation

The complete realization of this state beyond effort is through the perfection of the process of self-liberation, which develops through three stages according to the capacity of the individual:

❋ The first stage of self-liberation is compared to a dewdrop evaporating when the warmth of the sun falls upon it.

❋ The second level is illustrated by the image of a snowflake melting into the surface of the sea.

❋ The final level is compared to that of a snake uncoiling a knot in its own body in an instant, thus liberating itself spontaneously.

By this point, any separation between a 'subject' and 'object' has dissolved and everything is said to be of 'one taste'. At this stage, all one's ordinary karmic visions and passions are said to be like an ornament of one's state, for they do not condition the individual but are instantly self-liberated.

'Seeing that everything is self-perfected
from the very beginning,
the disease of striving for any achievement
Comes to an end of its own accord,
And just remaining in the natural state as it is,
The presence of non-dual contemplation,
Continuously, spontaneously arises ...' [11]

The real manifestation of the fruit of Dzogchen practice is that of remaining in the natural state just 'as it is' throughout all one's activities: in one's daily life, while sleeping and ultimately beyond death itself.

PSYCHOTHERAPY AND THE BUDDHIST APPROACH

'What other method is there for liberation apart from knowing the nature of mind? If you do not know this key point of mind essence, then whatever you do misses the main point.' [12]

In order to apply the principles of Dzogchen, it is considered very important at the outset to differentiate clearly between the 'ordinary mind', which is involved in conceptual thinking and judging, and the 'nature of mind', the unborn mind essence. Before even approaching the essential nature of mind, with its perfect unchanging qualities, we first need to become familiar with the workings of our mind, with all its problems, limitations and constraints. If we do not deal with these issues directly then all we are doing is evading our real condition by convincing ourselves we are somehow 'above it' or 'beyond it'.

By looking into the mirror of our own mind in a very ordinary way, we begin to see our situation more clearly: who we think we are, how we habitually deal with life situations and how we interact with others. In this way we slowly begin to know ourselves a little better. By examining our daily behaviour, our thoughts, feelings and actions, we start to gain insight into the nature of our life and ourselves in a very practical way. By observing the type of problems we experience, we can also start to understand the causes of our difficulties and our limitations, and take steps to deal with them.

Of course, there are many ways of approaching a problem. The first step is that of admitting that we actually have a problem that needs to be dealt with. If we don't take that first step ourselves, there is nothing to be done – no one else can help. Self-reflection is therefore crucial in overcoming any kind of difficulty.

Once a problem has been identified or diagnosed, however, there are different types of remedy. Some are more far-reaching than others. Simply swallowing a sleeping pill to overcome anxiety and insomnia, for example, will help to deal with the problem in the short term, but the root of the difficulty will not have been dealt with. Psychotherapeutic approaches to mental stress or anxiety can go further in helping an individual to understand the nature of their problems and how to overcome them. But at a certain point even self-reflection has its limitations, because in this process there is still a division between an 'observer' and an 'observed'. And although a healthy ego has a valuable role to play in managing our everyday affairs, from the viewpoint of contemplation, it needs to be transcended. Ultimately, as the Buddha himself realized, the root of all our problems is our habitual way of seeing, our dualistic vision that separates 'me' from 'other', the 'possessor' from the 'possessed'.

'*From the perspective of contemplative practice, the root source of human suffering is this very split between "me" and "my experience". Suffering is nothing more than the observer judging, resisting, struggling with, and attempting to control experiences that are painful, scary, or threatening to it. Without that struggle, difficult experiences would be perceived more precisely as just what they are, instead of dire threats to the survival and integrity of "me". Conventional psychotherapy teaches clients to understand, manage and reduce the suffering that arises out of identification with a separate ego-self, but rarely questions the fundamental inner set up that gives rise to it.*' [13]

Most therapy, although not all (such as the Transpersonal approach and Jung's ideal of the undivided 'Self'), aims at reducing distress and increasing self-understanding within the limitations of conventional social structures rather than attempting to overcome 'divided consciousness' as such. Meditation, on the other hand, progressively helps us to let go of our habitual identification and attachment to experiences. This ultimately allows a pure awareness to arise which is intrinsically free of emotional compulsion or mental judgement.

'*... there is a time for actively trying to penetrate experiential obstacles and a time for allowing one's experience to be as it is. If we are unable or unwilling to actively engage with our personal life issues, then letting-be could become a stance of avoidance, and a dead-end. Yet if we are unable to let our experience be, or to open to it just as it is, then our psychological work may reinforce the habitual contraction of the conditioned personality.*' [14]

The wide range of psychotherapeutic approaches now on offer in the West certainly has a vital role to play in contemporary society where the modern pressures of living have left many individuals feeling morally, spiritually and socially alienated. However, to suggest that psychotherapy and spiritual practice are in some ways synonymous or interchangeable is misleading, not least because the terms 'meditation' and 'psychotherapy' are both used loosely to refer to a very diverse range of practices.

In recent years, there has been a tendency to experiment with combining certain Buddhist practices with psychotherapeutic techniques in an attempt to utilize the value of both approaches. Although it is important that a marriage takes place between the Western psyche and the essential elements of Buddhism, it is vital not to confuse the two and thereby dilute the integrity of each tradition.

'Western psychology's present love affair with the Orient seems to me … dangerous. The danger lies in the enormous power psychological ways of thinking now wield in our culture, a power so vast that the present psychologizing of Eastern contemplative disciplines – unless it is preceded by a thorough revolution in Western psychology itself – could rob these disciplines of their spiritual substance. It could pervert them into Western mental-health gimmicks and thereby prevent them from introducing the sharply alternative vision of life they are capable of bringing to us.' [15]

Traditional Buddhism, as already mentioned, speaks of both the 'ordinary mind' and of the underlying 'nature of mind': the former is prone to all sorts of anxieties and problems, while the latter is intrinsically free of all concepts being beyond the grasp of the intellect. In the context of the ordinary mind Buddhism embraces certain goals and ideas in common with the psychotherapeutic approach, but it is essentially a transmission of knowledge which goes beyond words, beyond mind and ulti-mately beyond self. As Chögyam Trungpa says:

'From the Buddhist point of view, there is a problem with any attempt to pinpoint, categorize, and pigeonhole mind and its con-tents very neatly. This method could be called psychological mate-rialism. The problem with this approach is that it does not leave enough room for spontaneity and openness. It overlooks basic healthiness ...' [16]

Ultimately, from the Dzogchen perspective, the nature of mind and the 'ordinary mind', are inseparable or 'non-dual'. In the self-perfected state, it is impossible to find even the smallest gap between a mirror and its reflections.

FOOTNOTES

[fn1] Samantabhadra is depicted as a blue unadorned Buddha but he is really a symbol of the *dharmakaya* and our own true nature.

CHAPTER 4

THE PRACTICE OF MEDITATION

'Someone who begins to develop an interest in the teachings can tend to distance themselves from the reality of material things, as if the teachings were something completely apart from daily life. Often at the bottom of this, there is an attitude of giving up and running from one's own problems, with the illusion that one will be able to find something that will miraculously help one to transcend all that. But the teachings are based on the principle of our actual human condition. We have a physical body with all its various limits: each day we have to eat, work, rest and so on. This is our reality, and we can't ignore it.' [1]

The very notion of being able to integrate the spiritual quest with everyday life has enormous value in contemporary Western society. Most people have families, jobs and social commitments, so it is not possible for them to dedicate themselves to long periods of formal practice, as was done in Tibet. The idea of being able to give up one's daily life to become a wandering yogi or spiritual sage hardly finds a ready place within our society.

Ani Tenzin Palmo, a Western nun who has spent much of her life in long retreat, intimately understands the dilemma which many Westerners face in practising *dharma* today:

'... *to always present the* dharma *as though* dharma *practice merely means sitting on your mat doing a strict practice ... and the rest of the time you're not doing that is not* dharma *practice is an incredible misconception and causes enormous frustration for people because they don't have the time ... because really* dharma *means an inner transformation of the mind ... it's not something we have to package into certain times of the day, it's something that should flow from us moment to moment to moment.'* [2]

Such an approach is also very valuable in helping overcome the duality of what is often perceived as a split between one's spiritual life on the one hand and one's secular life on the other. In other words, such a view helps to heal the division between the sacred and the profane, between spirit and matter, which is embedded deep in the subconscious psyche of most Westerners. According to Chögyal Namkhai Norbu:

'It's good to enjoy things, enjoy life. People think that leading a spiritual life means that you have to put yourself through great self-torture for the teaching ... but why? The point is good intention.' [3]

The real transformation has to take place internally. In any case, it is not so easy to escape from our problems by simply changing our outer circumstances or by adopting a new set of rules, because we simply tend to re-create the same kind of situation again in a different context.

Running away from the responsibilities and problems which are presented by daily life is one of the criticisms that is frequently directed at those who set out on a spiritual path. It is not unfounded. The various forms of asceticism or renunciation which are demanded by some types of religious practice often require some manner of withdrawal from worldly life and from conventional social interaction. The practice of Dzogchen, however, if correctly understood, does not correspond with this approach because the ability to integrate spiritual practice into one's everyday life is fundamental to this tradition. Like a pure lotus flower growing out of the mud, Dzogchen can be practised in the midst of the turmoil of daily life and does not require the individual to give up or change anything.

But if one does not need to change anything, what is there to do? In Dzogchen there is a wide range of different methods and specific practices, but methods from other teachings can also be used if appropriate.

'Dzogchen is like the highest point, the golden top-ornament: above it there is nothing but sky ...'[4]

The Dzogchen view of practice is considered to be like standing on the top of a mountain. When you stand on its peak, it is possible to see in all directions, yet this is not the case when you are only halfway up the mountain. This means that from the Dzogchen perspective, it is possible to see the relative role of all the other paths as well as understanding their value.

In fact, it is very helpful to be familiar with a wide range of different methods and know when it is appropriate to use them. This may include methods taken from the Sutra teachings or the Tantric path as well as from Dzogchen, or indeed any other approach which may be useful. A Dzogchen practitioner is entirely free about what to engage in. It is a matter of self-observation to discern what is necessary in a given situation, rather than following a set of rules.

'... if you practise the Dzogchen teachings, it does not mean that you are limited only to those teachings. Dzogchen is like a key

enabling you to enter every sort of teaching. When we do Dzogchen practice, the first thing we try to understand is the principle of the teaching and after that we integrate this with every sort of teaching that we use.'[5]

In practising some of the Tantras, for example, an individual is obliged to do certain things, such as recite a set number of mantras each day. A Dzogchen practitioner, however, is not obliged to do anything. According to the Dzogchen view, an individual uses certain practices when they see the need, rather than because a teacher tells them to do so. Otherwise there is the danger that they can become too dependent on that teacher. It is important to observe ourselves in order to understand what we need, rather than being dependent on anybody else.

Knowing which approach to employ at any given moment or how to respond to a certain situation is not always that straightforward. From the Dzogchen point of view, the governing principle is always individual 'awareness' rather than a set rule of behaviour. Each circumstance is different, each situation demands a different solution: what is right for me may not be right for you. We should simply try to do our best and follow our inclinations. At the same time, by engaging in different methods which help us to develop our clarity, we can deepen our understanding and insight.

PRINCIPAL AND SECONDARY PRACTICES

With regard to practice in Dzogchen, we start by observing ourselves. To discern what is appropriate for us, we need to be clear about our personal capacity and be honest with ourselves about our limitations. In order to know how to proceed, it is also very important to understand what the specific purpose of each practice is and why we are doing it.

In Dzogchen, an important distinction is made between principal practices and secondary practices. The principal practices are those which enable the individual to enter the non-dual state, or the state of contemplation, directly. Secondary practices are those which provide assistance on the path, using methods such as purification or transformation. The principal practices are like the trunk of a tree, whereas the secondary practices are like its branches.

Dzogchen differs from other Buddhist teachings in that it uses the method of Direct Introduction of the primordial state from the master to the student. This distinguishes it from other paths in Tibetan Buddhism where one progresses slowly through different levels of preliminary practice. Thus in Dzogchen a practitioner is given the opportunity to enter the practice at the highest level immediately, without any prerequisites. Other practices may then be used to overcome any obstacles or difficulties to contemplation that may arise subsequently.

Principal Practices

In Dzogchen, the principal practice is non-dual contemplation where one is not conditioned by the arising of thoughts. For this, transmission from a realized master is essential and the practice of *guru yoga* is indispensable. *Guru yoga* is the unification of one's own mind with that of the teacher and it is the key to realization and liberation, to the awakened state or Buddhahood. It is based on the principle of transmission, in that the teacher embodies the non-dual state of contemplation itself. The real primary practice is to continue in the state of contemplation, using *guru yoga* to develop one's practice. Thus the relationship with the teacher lies at the heart of Dzogchen practice.

Another principal practice in Dzogchen, taught widely by Chögyal Namkhai Norbu, works more specifically through sound. 'The Song of the Vajra' is a long melodious mantric chant which is sung in the language of the dakinis (manifestations of enlightened female energy). The emphasis is on the sound itself, rather than on the meaning of the words, for the very sound induces the state of contemplation which is beyond words, concepts or intellectual knowledge.

> 'Unborn, yet continuing without interruption,
> Neither coming nor going, omnipresent,
> Supreme dharma,
> Unchangeable space, without definition,
> Spontaneously self-liberating –
> Perfectly unobstructed state –
> Manifest from the very beginning,
> Self-created, without location,
> With nothing negative to reject,
> And nothing positive to accept,
> Infinite expanse, penetrating everywhere,
> Immense, and without limits, without ties,
> With nothing even to dissolve
> Or to be liberated from,
> Manifest beyond space and time,
> Existing from the beginning ...'[6]

Thus, although the words of 'The Song of the Vajra' do have a meaning, as seen above, the real sense of this mantra is to introduce or represent our fundamental dimension of the self-perfected state.

Connected with this song is a dance called the Dance of the Vajra, which was revealed to Chögyal Namkhai Norbu through a series of visionary dreams. Like 'The Song of the Vajra', the Dance of the Vajra is related to the state of contemplation and is therefore also a principal practice in Dzogchen.

Secondary Practices

There are a number of secondary practices which may be used by the Dzogchen practitioner. They are called 'secondary' because although they help to purify or clarify our condition and can provide a support on the path, they are still only a preparation for the main or primary practice. Some of these work specifically to purify obstacles, like the practice of Vajrasattva,[fn1] which is common to all the Tibetan traditions. There are also internal purification practices which are found particularly in Dzogchen. Other secondary practices can help to strengthen our life force or overcome illnesses such as cancer. Practices such as inner heat and others from the Six Yogas of Naropa[fn2] may also be used by Dzogchen practitioners as secondary practices.

Another example of a secondary practice is the traditional Buddhist method of performing prostrations, a type of physical 'prayer of action' which has the effect of purifying or clearing away obstacles and preparing the ground for other practices.

The Sutra teachings and lower Tantras place great emphasis on purification practices which focus on the body, voice and mind of the individual. In reality many practices work on all three 'doors' simultaneously, thereby increasing clarity and removing obstacles. In Dzogchen all these practices can be extremely useful, but they are not obligatory prerequisites for the Direct Introduction.

A dynamic system of yoga particular to Dzogchen, which works specifically with the body, speech and mind, is Yantra Yoga. It is a secondary practice in that it allows the practitioner to enter more easily into the state of contemplation. Known as the 'Union of the Sun and Moon Yantra', it has been taught continuously from the time of the famous translator Vairocana in the eighth century AD until today. It was Vairocana who wrote down the Yantra Yoga teachings, which have 108 principal positions. Divided into five different groups, they each control breathing in different ways.

A practice popular among many contemporary Dzogchen practitioners and great masters of the past is that of Chod. This is a powerful practice for overcoming attachment which was propagated by the female teacher Machig Labdron more than 1,000 years ago. It incorporates elements of Sutra, Tantra and Dzogchen and is aimed at cutting through attachment to the ego directly. Traditionally practised in charnel grounds to arouse intense fear in the practitioner, Chod works melodiously with the sound of the voice, drums, a thigh-bone trumpet and a bell. The practitioner visualizes the offering of their body to a host of invited guests. It is a dynamic and vigorous practice and thus appeals quite strongly to Westerners' desire to be active. From the point of view of Dzogchen it is useful because it helps us to overcome attachment to what we hold most dear, i.e. our own body.

For a newcomer to Dzogchen, there may seem to be such a wide array of practices as to make it quite bewildering. It is important, therefore, never to forget the main point of Dzogchen practice and realize that all these different methods are simply available to be used in the appropriate circumstances.

According to Chögyal Namkhai Norbu:

'... *Dzogchen practitioners can also do* pujas *[rites] if they like, but this is not a principal practice. The only thing you must try to do is* Guruyoga.'[7]

The essence, then, of all Dzogchen practice is to be in the state of non-dual contemplation and to integrate this with all one's activities. This is what is meant by 'conduct' or 'behaviour' on the path, i.e. the ability to integrate one's experience of contemplation beyond a formal session of meditation and into daily life.

'*The teachings must become a living knowledge in all one's daily activities. This is the essence of the practice, and besides that there is nothing in particular to be done.*'[8]

Or, in the words of Patrul Rinpoche:

'*Don't entertain thoughts about what has passed, don't anticipate or plan what will happen in the future. Leave your present wakefulness unaltered, utterly free and open. Aside from that, there is nothing else whatsoever to do!*'[9]

MINDFULNESS AND THE STATE OF INSTANT PRESENCE

'*Many people consider practice is chanting mantras or sitting doing some rituals, etc. This is practice, but not the main practice. The main practice is first of all to discover our "instant presence" and then to integrate that state in any moment. It is not so easy to always be in "instant presence", but when we have the possibility we try. We try to be aware and not distracted and try to be aware in our life and circumstances.'*[10]

The ability to integrate practice into daily life in this way requires careful preparation through a process of familiarization with the exact experience of the state of instant presence, or *rigpa*.

It is important to make a distinction between meditation and contemplation. The principal practice in Dzogchen is that of non-dual contemplation, in which thought automatically liberates itself. In a state of contemplation, the practitioner will have thoughts but is not conditioned by them. This is the key to Dzogchen practice and from this point of view there is nothing to do. Meditation, however, involves working with the mind using some of the numerous practices available in order to enter the state of contemplation.

Most approaches to formal meditation practice start by training an individual to observe their thoughts and to watch the movements of their mind. By fixing the attention on the breath or on an external object, such as a candle or an image, the mind naturally begins to become calmer and more transparent. When the movements of the mind become still, then it can be compared to the placid surface of a pool where the water is so clear that you can see right beneath the surface and into the depths.

A natural result of observing the mind is that we gain greater insight into its unconscious contents, which are not so apparent when we are immersed in our daily activities. We are also less distracted by thoughts when they arise. In Dzogchen, this practice is known as 'fixation with an object' and its aim is to induce a calm state. It is a practice found in all Buddhist schools of meditation and is known as *shine* meditation, the calm state of meditation.

Once the practice of fixation with an object is stabilized, the fixation is relaxed and one moves on to 'fixation without an object'. In this practice, a practitioner gazes at a wall or into the open space of the sky. Now there is no focal point on which to anchor the mind, allowing a greater sense of freedom and space.

Once a state of calm has been reached through fixation practices, automatically the state of intuitive clarity, or *lhagthong*, arises. In Dzogchen *lhagthong* refers to the ability to integrate movement with the state of presence. This means that a practitioner is not disturbed by noise or external interruptions and does not require a quiet isolated place in which to practise. At this point contemplation can be applied in daily life.

Both *shine* and *lhagthong* are considered principal practices in Dzogchen, as they bring the practitioner into the state of contemplation.

'The mind itself is vast and unchanging as the sky. A spacious and unpredictable dance of magical compassion: what else could all this be but an ornament of absolute space? Whether things are inside or outside, gathering or dispersing, it is all the play of the compassionate mind. Once we understand that reality is not fixed, then we can make anything of it. What a wonderful play of magical illusion. How amazing and admirable a phenomenon it is!' [11]

In everyday life, attention or alert mindfulness can be continued beyond the formal meditation session and into daily life by maintaining a continuity of watchfulness. Here the mind is still maintaining a degree of 'attention', although it is more subtle and diffuse in nature. In other words, there is still an element of control. Cultivating a continuity of mindfulness or presence and awareness in our daily activities, such as shopping, walking or driving a car, is a very useful and practical exercise. It is also a very valuable method of training or preparing for integrating 'instant presence' into our lives. Mindfulness, however, always implies some kind of division between the 'observer' and the 'observed', whereas with instant presence this duality does not exist.

'It is very important in daily life to be aware and not to be distracted … but this is not instant presence; being present means we have a kind of attention. Instant presence has no attention, it is beyond attention; but if you are present with attention then it is very easy to integrate this into instant presence.' [12]

To be in the state of instant presence, or *rigpa*, is to be beyond having to apply any kind of attention or effort. In Tibetan, it is symbolized by the letter 'ༀ' (in English 'A'). It has no distinguishing characteristic other than its own inherent wakefulness. There is nothing to change, modify or apply – the only practice is to be in the condition 'as it is'.

'You must understand that to do Dzogchen practice it is not necessary to do three or seven years of retreat somewhere, closing yourself up. But it is most important to train yourself, to go somewhere quiet and do practice. Then when you have had exact experience of the state of rigpa, *then you integrate this understanding with your existence. Existence here means you have a body with its movements, your speech and also your mind, your thoughts. And slowly, slowly, you integrate all your movements in the state of* rigpa. *So to have the possibility of integration, it is not necessary that you go to some special place or do some complicated practice. You can always do practice and practice can become your life: your movements, thoughts, etc. Everything can be integrated with this practice.'* [13]

Spending a certain amount of time in solitude or in a retreat situation is, however, vital for initially discovering and later developing the state of instant presence. This is the key to Dzogchen practice. By just being in a quiet place where all the usual distractions are absent, it is much easier for our habitual mental constructs to diminish, for the mind to become more peaceful and for us to reawaken to a natural simplicity of being.

*'You simply need to **allow** the moment of uncontrived naturalness. Instead of meditating upon it, meaning focusing, simply allow it to naturally be. The words for "training" and "meditating" sound the same in Tibetan, so to play on that … It is more a matter of familiarization than meditation … The more you grow familiar with mind essence, the less you deliberately meditate upon it, the easier it becomes to recognize and the simpler to sustain.'* [14]

There is a famous saying: 'By abandoning activities, we approach the nature of non-doing.' Yet once this effortless state has been discovered, the real challenge is that of learning how to integrate this precious living experience into the more mundane round of daily life. We need to have stabilized the contemplative experience within ourselves in a very real way before returning to the marketplace.

THE ART OF NON-DOING

'In fact there is nothing to be done, so we may abide in non-action, beyond both action and non-action. We already have this perfect unchanging nature, so why try to perfect ourselves, purify ourselves, attend to a teacher and go along a path? This question inevitably arises.' [15]

Since we are already enlightened from the very beginning, why do we need to do anything? It is easy to misunderstand the Dzogchen teachings. Although our primordial nature is pure from the very beginning, it is like a clear blue sky obscured by clouds of our own ignorance. In fact, a practitioner of Dzogchen should ceaselessly try to discover *rigpa*, or the state of contemplation, and to learn what it means to integrate this knowledge into their daily life, whatever the circumstances. We need to discriminate between our primordial state and our conditioned existence.

'*As space pervades, awareness pervades. Like space,* rigpa *is all-encompassing, nothing is outside it. Just as the world and beings are pervaded by space, [so]* rigpa *pervades the minds of all beings ...* '[16]

If we pretend that we are enlightened and that everything is perfect when it is not, we are simply deluding ourselves. Moreover, simply to drop all our attachments and walk away from the cage of our conditioning is difficult and generally needs to be accomplished by degrees.

'*Paradoxically it is hard to allow the innate completion of "perfection" of experience. Just to relax and let the world reveal itself is difficult. The fear of annihilation of the constructed self is hard to overcome, for in fact it is only "overcome" by surrendering to it, allowing its presence ... This is not the state of a subject inside looking at an object world "out there". The experience of this is not attainable through words, for it is not a position to be defined and adhered to.*'[17]

But even if it is difficult for us to overcome all our limitations in an instant, it is important to remember that there is always the possibility of rediscovering our true nature. The famous vagabond Patrul Rinpoche proclaimed: 'Beyond both action and inaction, the supreme Dharma is accomplished. So simply preserve the state and rest your weary mind.' [18] But his disciple Khenpo Ngawang Palzang said: 'Dzogchen is extremely simple, but not easy,' [19] while Jigme Lingpa, another of the great Dzogchen masters commented: 'Teachings about Dzogchen are many. Knowers of Dzogchen are few ...' [20]

The path of Dzogchen may sound easy – but it is not! When it is described as the path of 'non-doing' or 'non-meditation', this has to be understood in the correct context. The fact remains that most of the great Dzogchen masters spent many years in solitary retreat. On one famous occasion the great Dzogchen practitioner Yungton Dorje Pal was questioned about his practice:

Monk: *'Oh, you are a practitioner of Dzogchen, you must meditate all the time.'*
Yungton Dorje Pal: *'What am I meditating on?'*
Monk: *'So, you practitioners of Dzogchen do not do any meditation?'*
Yungton Dorje Pal: *'When am I distracted?'* [21]

Having nothing to meditate on implies that one has already understood and completely integrated one's daily existence into the state 'beyond activity'. One simply resides in the natural state with an attitude of relaxation.

Being relaxed, however, doesn't mean laziness. The story of Milarepa, the great eleventh-century yogi, and his encounter with the Dzogchen master Lama Rongton Llaga illustrates this. The master had told Milarepa that for exceptionally gifted or fortunate disciples it was possible to gain liberation immediately on simply hearing about Dzogchen, without having to do anything!

> *'In one moment, perfect recognition,*
> *In one instant, complete enlightenment.'*[22]

Convinced that he was one of the gifted ones, Milarepa thought that he could obtain freedom without having to practise at all. He therefore spent most of his time sleeping. When, after a few days, the master came to see how he was getting on, he saw straightaway that Milarepa was too lazy and conceited to make any effort at all. Throwing up his hands in disgust, he cried:

'You introduced yourself as a doomed man and it's clearly true. My own pride made me agree too quickly to help you. I obviously gave you instructions in the path of "The Great Perfection" before you were ready. Now I see that there is nothing I can do to help you.'[23]

This, of course, was the cue for him to send Milarepa on his way to meet his predestined teacher Marpa the Translator, under whose strict supervision he endured many years of hardship. The relationship between Milarepa and his teacher Marpa is the most famous of all Tibetan folk tales. It illustrates, above all, the vital importance within the Tibetan Buddhist tradition of finding an authentic teacher. This is seen as absolutely fundamental to the discovery of the state of knowledge.

FOOTNOTES

[fn1] Vajrasattva (Skt) (Tib. *rdo rje sems dpa'*): *Vajra* means the primordial state of enlightenment. *Sattva* means a great being with this knowledge. Vajrasattva is white in colour and the practice of Vajrasattva is especially important for purification.

[fn2] The Six Yogas of Naropa are six yogic practices found in the Karma Kagyud school: Inner Heat (*gtum mo*), the Illusory Body (*sgyu lus*), Dream (*rmi lam*), Clear Light (*'od gsal*), Intermediate States (*bar do*) and the Transference of Consciousness (*'pho ba*).

CHAPTER 5

THE VALUE OF AN AUTHENTIC TEACHER

'Milarepa sang, "When I am alone, meditating in the mountains, all the Buddhas past, present and future are with me. Guru Marpa is always with me. All beings are here."' [1]

In Dzogchen, the heart of the teachings lies in the relationship with the teacher, or guru. The term 'guru', however, has become contentious in the West following considerable exposure during the last two decades of sexual, financial or political impropriety on the part of teachers in a number of spiritual traditions, including Buddhism. As a result it has acquired negative connotations that do not exist in Eastern traditions. Although critical analysis is a necessary counterbalance to the initial naïvety on the part of Westerners towards spiritual teachers from the East, unfortunately it has also given rise to a great deal of misunderstanding about the nature of the teacher/student relationship. Particularly in America, feminist doubts about following what is often conceived as a patriarchal spiritual structure have gained ground in recent years and pose some very real questions in a world of evolving equality. In some quarters there has even been a move to dispense entirely with the concept of the teacher or guru. There is a danger that this view, a currently fashionable one, can be critically misleading and provide an erroneous basis for the development of Tibetan Buddhism, where the relationship with the teacher is critically important for spiritual development. It is also important to understand that the state of enlightenment is free from notions of gender.

> 'Because the expanse of reality is not "I",
> It is not a "woman", not a "man".
> It is completely freed from all grasping.
> How could it be designated as an "I"?
>
> In all phenomena without attachment
> Neither woman, nor man are conceived.
> To tame those who are blinded by desire
> A "woman" and a "man" are taught.'[2]

The Sanskrit word *guru* literally means 'master'. In Tibetan this is translated as *lama* (*bla ma*). *Bla* means 'the vital principle of life is energy' and *ma* means 'the potency of mother'. *Lama* means therefore 'life-mother' or 'spiritual master'. According to Patrul Rinpoche, 'There is nothing higher.'[3] *Ma*, meaning 'mother', implies a mother looking over a child's growth. In this sense a superior spiritual being is looking after one's growth, guiding one to liberation. Fortunately for Tibetan Buddhism, the term 'lama' has not acquired the negative overtones of the term 'guru'.

The need for a teacher is stressed not only in Buddhist teachings but also in other religions. For the Sufis, with their emphasis on the heart, the link with the teacher is vital, and for Hindus a living teacher is necessary so that knowledge does not stay on an intellectual level.

How then are Westerners to reconcile the two extremes of uncritical devotion to a teacher with the critical intellectual analysis necessary for understanding? For those sincere about following spiritual teachings, there needs to be an understanding of the crucial role of the teacher in Tibetan Buddhist traditions, and particularly in Dzogchen. Secondly, close observation and critical evaluation of a teacher are needed before committing oneself wholeheartedly to a spiritual path. In the end, each person is responsible for their own realization.

TAKING REFUGE

A fundamental notion in Buddhism is that of going for refuge. The reason one goes for refuge is to overcome suffering. There are two kinds of refuge: the first is a provisional or temporary refuge in a worldly sense, such as taking shelter in a house during a storm, and the second is the absolute or definitive refuge, where one takes refuge in the Three Jewels, the Buddha, Dharma and Sangha,[fn1] until one no longer dwells in a state of duality, the root of all suffering, and attains complete realization.

The teacher is considered more important than the Buddha, Dharma or Sangha, for without the teacher there would be no Buddha or access to the lineage of Buddhas, no Dharma, no teachings, and no Sangha, or community of practitioners, for these cannot exist in isolation without the master. The teacher in fact *is* the Buddha, Dharma and Sangha and the gateway to realization.

The lama 'brings us the transmission of the Buddhas of the past, embodies for us the Buddhas of the present, and through his teaching, is the source of the Buddhas of the future'.[4]

Changchub Dorje said:

'The Lama and One's Mind and Buddha, these three: in any moment, recognize that they are the same thing, there is no difference

*between them … there is no difference between all these three,
even if we consider them as three separate things.'[5]*

The very short and direct path of Dzogchen in particular requires
an authentic qualified teacher to introduce the student directly to
their own Buddha nature. This can only be done through a
teacher who has realized their own self-perfected nature. Although
we all have this potential, this 'Buddha nature' which can ripen
into complete enlightenment, without a teacher it is difficult to
have direct access to the wisdom of the Buddhas, as our own wisdom and clarity are not yet sufficiently developed.

*'Although the Buddhas are all enlightened and full of wisdom,
without a teacher, that **wisdom is too weak**.'[6]*

Choosing a teacher is therefore of paramount importance.

> *'Just as the trunk of an ordinary tree
> Lying in the forests of the Malaya mountains
> Absorbs the perfume of sandal from the moist leaves
>   and branches,
> So you come to resemble whomever you follow.'[7]*

FINDING A TEACHER

So how does one find a fully qualified and authentic teacher?
In an age of false prophets and self-proclaimed gurus, a certain
amount of discernment and caution is necessary to protect
aspiring spiritual practitioners.

There are a number of ways of checking a teacher. A true
teacher should be pure, with full realization of the path of

liberation they are teaching. They should embody both morality and deep learning as well as having actualized the authentic state of *samadhi*.[fn2]

Crucially, they should also have a heart suffused with loving kindness and compassion (even wrathful compassion where necessary). It was said of Patrul Rinpoche, who practised loving kindness, or *bodhicitta*, as his main practice, that such was the strength of his practice that whenever he taught the classic Buddhist text by Shantideva, the *Bodhicaryavatara*, 'A Guide to the Bodhisattva's Way of Life', special flowers would blossom.

The Dalai Lama is a shining contemporary example of a deeply compassionate human being who touches all those who meet him, regardless of their spiritual or religious affiliation. For him, 'our basic nature is that of love and compassion ... In human nature there is a natural feeling for living things.'[8]

The great yogi Shabkar Rinpoche[fn3] sings:

> '*If a man has compassion, he is Buddha*
> *Without compassion, he is Lord of Death ...*
>
> *Great compassion is like a wish-fulfilling gem.*
> *Great compassion fulfills the hopes of self and others.*
>
> *Therefore, all of you, renunciants and householders,*
> *Cultivate compassion and you will achieve Buddhahood.*'[9]

A very important thing is to rely upon the teachings and examine them carefully. The Buddha himself emphasized careful scrutiny of the teachings: 'As a goldsmith would test his gold by burning, cutting, and rubbing it, so you must examine my words and accept them, but not merely out of reverence for me.'[10]

Chögyal Namkhai Norbu, however, warns that in Dzogchen:

'... *you shouldn't even be too dependent on the master. The master is important because he has communicated and I have understood and integrated with my knowledge. But that doesn't mean that he has become the boss and that I am dependent on him ... As far as realization is concerned, the most important thing is that a master exists who communicates the way to be followed.*'[11]

Sometimes Westerners find that they have committed themselves to a Tibetan Buddhist teacher only to discover that either their ethics are questionable, that they are too autocratic or that their teachings are divisive and sectarian in terms of the larger Buddhist community. This can pose very serious problems for a sincere practitioner. In such cases, it is perfectly in order to move to another teacher, maintaining respect for the teacher one has left and discarding those teachings that are not useful.

DIFFERENT KINDS OF TEACHER

'To meet a perfect teacher
Is more valuable than gaining a kingdom.
Look how those with no devotion
Treat the teacher as their equal!

To see the real nature of mind
Is more valuable than meeting the Buddha.
Look how those who have no determination
Drift back into delusion!'[12]

According to Chögyal Namkhai Norbu, there are four different types of teacher. The first is the one who helps you onto the path in a very fundamental way by teaching you to read, as this is 'relevant to eventually awakening you', or it may be someone who's written a book. The second type of teacher plants the seed of faith. The third type of teacher relates to teachers in the lineage, even those you have never met, i.e. the teacher of your teacher. It also includes teachers who give transmission through mantra.

There is a remarkable story about a teacher in the Shangpa Kagyud[fn4] tradition called Tulku Ugyanpa who fits into the third category of teachers. It is said that he had 'hundreds of disciples who achieved full realization whom he had never met ... many many of these disciples obtained transmission from him and later achieved realization through letters that he wrote ... He never even spoke to these people.' [13]

The fourth category of teacher is the most important: the heart teacher known as the root lama, or *tsawai lama*. This is the teacher who makes you really understand the profound sense of the teachings but 'a root master is not something you choose ... He is that teacher who has brought me real knowledge, knowledge of the kind that we speak of as Direct Introduction ...' [14]

Obviously, meeting the root lama is most important for spiritual development, for it is the root lama who opens one's eyes, and one meets one's root master at the particular moment when it's appropriate to do so.

Tenzin Palmo is a contemporary outstanding Englishwoman who spent more than 12 years in retreat in a cave, hidden and isolated in the Lahoul mountains in northern India. For her, the meeting with her root teacher, Khamtrul Rinpoche, was down to earth and understated, yet marked by a sure sense of recognition. Just the sound of his name reverberated immediately with her.

'*The feeling was two things at the same time. One was seeing somebody you knew extremely well whom you haven't seen for a very long time. A feeling of "Oh, how nice to see you again!" and at the same time it was as though an innermost part of my being had taken form in front of me.*'[15]

The great eleventh-century yogi Milarepa, beloved as a folk hero and saint equally amongst both Tibetans and Westerners, was profoundly affected by his meeting with his root teacher, Marpa. After practising black magic against his relatives in revenge for them misappropriating his family's land and wealth, and successfully killing 35 people at his cousin's wedding feast, he finally saw the enormity of his actions and repented.

In an effort to overcome his great suffering and purify his negative actions, he was sent to meet a famous Dzogchen master, but, as already explained, not realizing what a valuable opportunity this was, he spent most of his time sleeping! The Dzogchen master, fed up with his arrogance and laziness, finally told him to leave. 'I see that there is nothing I can do to help you. You should go to the great master Marpa, with whom I feel you have a natural connection through past lives.'

As soon as Milarepa heard the name 'Marpa', in his words, '... a shiver went through my spine and my hair stood on end. I was filled with a sudden longing to meet him face-to-face. Unable to think of anything else, I immediately set off for the southern Wheat Valley where he lived.'

Milarepa endured enormous hardships at the hand of his teacher. Marpa made him build a tower, only to have him knock it down and rebuild it in a different shape and another place! This happened a number of times until Milarepa, tested to breaking point and in a state of total despair, was on the brink of suicide. He had given up all hope of ever receiving teachings from Marpa when he was invited to a ceremony by his teacher. Marpa addressed the guests at the ceremony: 'Although I may have appeared unreasonable, I am not to blame for the Great Magician's suffering. In fact I used my rage as a skilful tool of guidance to test him thoroughly and to purify him of his past ill-deeds.'

Marpa then told Milarepa how he knew he would be a worthy disciple at their first meeting. 'When you drank all the beer I offered and finished ploughing the field, I knew for certain that you would be able to take in and understand the full meaning of the teaching and transmission. I put you through a series of gruelling ordeals yet you never lost faith or had ill thoughts about me ... Through you, the precious teachings will grow and flourish like the waxing moon.' [16]

THE STRENGTH OF PURE DEVOTION

'Better than meditating on a hundred thousand deities
For ten million kalpas
Is to think of one's teacher for a single instant.' [17]

When the disciple is fully prepared and ready, pure devotion to a realized being can bring instant realization. One of the most famous teachers of Dzogchen is Jigme Lingpa, who lived in the eighteenth century. When he first saw the writings of Longchenpa, another great Tibetan sage, who lived 400 years previously, he had a profound visionary experience: 'It dawned on me that he was genuinely a Buddha, and I prayed to him with great fervour. He appeared to me in a vision and accepted me.' [18]

Although he had not shown much interest in study while in the monastery, Jigme Lingpa became a great scholar and scientist through the strength of his meditation practice and devotion, which led to the awakening of his wisdom mind:

'Spontaneous realization was born within me and from that day forth, I have guided over a hundred disciples ... The way they all realized the ultimate truth came from the force of their devotion alone.' [19]

His main disciple was Jigme Gyalwai Nyugu, who in turn became the root guru of Patrul Rinpoche. Jigme Gyalwai Nyugu lived in a state of extreme simplicity, eating only wild plants. Not even having a cave for shelter, he slept in a hollow in the ground on the side of a remote mountain. After practising Dzogchen in such a fashion for a few years, he realized the absolute nature of mind through praying with intense devotion to Jigme Lingpa and the lineage of masters. So intensely did he pray that he became unconscious! On awakening, his mind and that of his lama had mingled to become inseparable in the state of primordial awareness. Such is the power of devotion that later he could understand all the teachings of the Buddha without even being taught.

For the young Dodrupchen Rinpoche[fn5] awakening came at the early age of 12 when his teacher asked him to drink a skull-cup of wine. Although he felt that he ought not to drink because of his monastic vows, out of pure devotion to his teacher, whom he viewed as a living Buddha, he drank the wine and was granted the great gift of understanding Dzogchen:

'Today the Buddha in person turned this monk
inside out and upside down,
and I have understood the essence of Dzogpa Chenpo,
the innate Great Perfection.' [20]

CHÖGYAL NAMKHAI NORBU AND CHANGCHUB DORJE

Sometimes the significant meeting with the root master is pre-saged in dreams.

'... I was brought to Changchub Dorje by a dream. I'm quite sure
that if I had never had that dream I never would have gone to
Changchub Dorje because there are hundreds of masters better
known than Changchub Dorje and considered more important.' [21]

Two years before Chögyal Namkhai Norbu met Changchub Dorje, he had an elaborate and vivid dream. In that dream he was in a village in which there were many houses built of white concrete. They were not Tibetan houses but more like Chinese buildings, which the Chinese had already started building in eastern Tibet. Above one of the doors was some large Tibetan script in gold letters on a blue background with the mantra of Padmasambhava. Entering this house, Chögyal Namkhai Norbu saw an old man with long hair, who appeared to be a simple ordinary Tibetan countryman. After greeting him, this old man began reciting the mantra of Padmasambhava. He then asked Chögyal Namkhai Norbu to visit a cave on the other side of the mountain, a cave which had eight *mandalas*[fn6], of the Kagyad (Northern Treasure) school[fn7], that had arisen naturally in the rock. With his father following him and both reciting the

Prajnaparamitra sutra, they were able to see parts of these eight *mandalas* but not all complete. Still reciting the Sutra, Chögyal Namkhai Norbu awoke.

Later, he heard of a famous doctor, an old countryman who lived in a village with houses made of white concrete. Apparently he was not just a doctor, he was an extraordinary being whose place was surrounded by white *stupas* or *chortens*[fn8] that were made in many strange shapes unlike elsewhere in Tibet. Chögyal Namkhai Norbu visited with his father and 'when we reached the master's village, I noticed that the place was exactly as I had seen it in my dream. The master welcomed us as if he already knew us …'[22] That is how I met that teacher and it seemed to me as if I already knew him. So right from the start I had no doubt at all.'[23]

Accustomed to living in a monastery and being given teachings in a traditional way, Chögyal Namkhai Norbu asked Changchub Dorje for a certain formal initiation, which he refused to give, saying that this was not the principle of the Dzogchen teachings. After much insistence, however, he finally agreed. This initiation could have been given in a very short time by an accomplished master, but Changchub Dorje was not an elegant master and had not had a formal education. As he could not read the text by himself, nor was used to performing rituals, the initiation took all day and half the night. He did not know the tunes or how to use the bell and drum correctly and 'he stumbled through the initiation'.[24] Chögyal Namkhai Norbu said that he himself was 'almost in a state of shock ... as I knew very well how an initiation should be done, and it was nothing like this'.[25] Finally, around midnight, for about three or four hours Changchub Dorje spoke uninterruptedly, as if he were reading from a text, and explained the real meaning of the Dzogchen teachings. Despite all his earlier misgivings, Chögyal

Namkhai Norbu's previous intellectual knowledge was now in tatters. He now understood that despite all he had learned before, he had never really entered into the true meaning of the teaching.

'I was greatly confused by this because then I knew that until then I had understood nothing of the teaching ... I truly understood what my own condition was ... Finally I understood that right from the beginning, when I first went to this teacher, he was giving me teachings. In the relationship with the teacher, when I was with him, everything that he said and did in daily life was pure teaching. After this I read many books ... and everything had a different taste and I understood that I had never understood the meaning before.' [26]

THE ABSOLUTE TEACHER

Saraha sang, 'In the ten directions, wherever I look, there is nothing besides this primordial Buddha, which has no arms and no legs, is just one infinite, luminous sphere.' [27]

In Dzogchen everything is the enlightened display of energy of the teacher, of the Buddha-mind. When finally the recognition dawns that one is inseparable from the enlightened mind, inseparable from the Buddha, and one's mind is completely saturated with the Buddha-mind of the teacher, then every moment becomes perfect and every experience is good. This is the state of *Samantabhadra*, which literally means 'All Good', a state in which there is no *samsara* from which to be liberated nor any *nirvana* to be attained. This is the teacher without form, the absolute teacher.

'Self-arising wisdom, primordially empty, is in a condition similar to space, and it pervades all beings without distinction, from glorious Samantabhadra *down to the tiniest insect on a blade of grass. For this reason the total state of* dharmakaya, *the inseparability of the two truths, absolute and relative, is called "the primordial Buddha"...'* [28]

Being in the state of *Samantabhadra* without effort is to be in the state of Dzogchen, the Great Perfection. All of existence is Dzogchen. This is the primordial lama from whom we are never separate and to whom we are introduced by an authentic and enlightened teacher.

'... Buddha, what is Buddha? We are the Buddha.' [29]

'What we have to understand ... is that the centre of the universe is our own state and there's nothing more important than that.' [30]

Ultimately, then, the teacher is not a personality to be glorified. The teacher represents the state of enlightenment that is within ourselves, i.e. the state of Buddhahood, rather than something that exists outside ourselves. But without access to the teacher, without union with their realized mind, without *guru yoga*, the teachings remain at a theoretical level.

FOOTNOTES

[fn1] Many Buddhist prayers start with taking refuge in the Three Jewels, paying homage to the Buddha, then to the Dharma, or the teachings, and thirdly to the Sangha, the monastic community or community of practitioners.

[fn2] *Samadhi* (Skt *dhyana*; Tib. *ting nge 'dzin*) or *samten* (*bSam gtan*): Meditative stability or concentration.

[fn3] Shabkar Rinpoche (1781–1851) is one of the most famous yogins of Tibet after

Milarepa. He was a Dzogchen practitioner who attained enlightenment in one lifetime and is renowned for his spiritual songs.

[fn4] Shangpa Kagyud (*shangs pa bka' brgyud*) is a lineage in the Kagyud school of Tibetan Buddhism which emphasizes meditation and includes the Six Yogas of Niguma (an eleventh-century yogini and companion or sister of Naropa).

[fn5] The fourth Dodrupchen Rinpoche, 1927–1961.

[fn6] Mandala (Skt) (Tib. *dkyil 'khor*): A complex visual manifestation of a deity (and its dimension) or a form of enlightenment.

[fn7] Kagyed (*bka' brgyad*): Eight *sadhana* teachings belonging to the Northern Treasure school of the Nyingmapa.

[fn8] *Stupa* (Skt) (Tib. *chorten; mchod rten*): Stupa, pagoda, funeral monument, receptacle of offerings, reliquary.

CHAPTER 6

GURU YOGA AND TRANSMISSION

'If there were no guruyoga *and transmission, then what is called the teaching of Dzogchen would become something like a philosophy.'*[1]

Guru yoga is the union of one's own mind with that of the teacher. It is the key to Buddhahood and to one's own realization. This happens through the transmission of knowledge from the teacher, who has in turn received the transmission from their teacher and so on, as though in a family line, except that this is a spiritual line or lineage of realization. Without this living link with the teacher who is the gateway to the teachings and lineage of masters, Dzogchen would remain a dry and academic source of study. The juice would be missing and there would be no possibility of the realization of the state of the Great Perfection. The teacher and lineage of transmission are, therefore, at the very heart of these teachings.

UNION WITH THE TEACHER

In Dzogchen, the emphasis on the practice of unifying one's mind with the teacher cannot be stressed enough. Its importance lies in the fact that it reawakens the state of primordial perfection within the practitioner and is therefore indispensable. It is *the* key to unlocking and developing knowledge and experience of the realized mind which is innate in all of us. This practice is known as *guru yoga*, union with the teacher. In Dzogchen, however,

'The ultimate meaning of guruyoga *is the unification of the state of consciousness of the master and oneself ... what's important is the final method, the real sense of the practice ... the teaching ... must take you to the state of the individual himself.'*[2]

Guru yoga is not done out of obligation towards the teacher but out of an obligation to developing our own spiritual realization. In this sense it has nothing to do with blind devotion or guru worship. It is like making offerings, whether actual or symbolic, to all the Buddhas. The Buddhas hardly need our offerings to improve their situation, but offering can be a training both for purifying our intention and developing generosity. It is therefore useful for our own development and growth.

Similarly, the practice of *guru yoga* is not done because the teacher needs our friendship or devotion:

'... you don't do guruyoga *out of affection for the teachers. Guruyoga is done to develop and deepen the transmission for the individual him or herself.'*[3]

The way we view the master is paramount, however, as it determines our level of realization. Padmasambhava himself said:

'If a practitioner views the master, the transmitter of the lineage, as a totally realized being – a Buddha – then he can become a Buddha. If the Guru is seen as a normal teacher, then the one who

sees him this way will realize the state of normal person. If seen as a little dog, he will obtain the realization of a dog.' [4]

In Dzogchen, *guru yoga* can also be a method of unifying all the teachings one has received and fulfilling obligations. In the West, particularly in the early heady days of the 1970s, many students went from teacher to teacher, drawn by the exoticism and outward display of richness and splendour of Tibetan Buddhism. Tibetan lamas very willingly gave out initiations and teachings, which almost inevitably carried with them a commitment to practise those teachings, usually including lengthy daily mantric recitation. This commitment is known as *samaya*, which means 'a spiritual pledge', 'a sacred vow or obligation'. *Samaya* subsequently became a major cause for neurosis in enthusiastic Westerners, who would now have to devote most of their days to fulfilling their sacred vows. There was no longer any time to work and lead a normal life if one did all the practices one had promised to do! This led to many difficulties for sincere students. The principle that all obligations can be fulfilled through the practice of *guru yoga* was never made clear. In Dzogchen this principle is explicit.

In Dzogchen, *guru yoga* can be practised in a very simple way which can take a few seconds or it can happen instantly. There are also methods in which it can be done slightly more elaborately, but the principle is always the same. As a practice it can be done very easily in the middle of a busy city life in less time than it takes to smoke a cigarette! It resolves all obligations to all one's previous teachers, whether Buddhist or not, dispels any guilt that might have been incurred through unfulfilled obligations and, crucially, it develops one's meditation and realization.

Furthermore, there is no longer the notion that some teachers are superior to others and some are lower and not worthy of such consideration; in one Tantra of Dzogchen, it even says that one can do *guru yoga* practice with the image of one's enemy as a way of overcoming the limitations of attachment and aversion! In Dzogchen, all teachers are united in a single figure or syllable without differentiation. The importance is the unification of the transmissions and keeping alive these transmissions at the heart of one's very being. This is the fuel for our realization.

'All transmissions are linked to knowledge. The ultimate transmissions are all on this level of Dzogchen. So we must unite all the different transmissions we've received – and which master it is is not important. Nor is it important to establish whether one master is better than another and should be treated better than another.' [5]

The most profound *guru yoga*, though, is not even an active practice, for it is said that the true *guru yoga* is the state of contemplation, the most powerful of all purifications. The Buddha said in the *Lankavatara sutra*[fn1] that even a brief moment of contemplation is worth infinitely more than a lifetime of collecting merit by doing good deeds or reciting sacred mantra. This is the way to enter the state of knowledge, the real meaning of the teachings.

The danger in modern Western society is that many self-appointed teachers give spiritual teachings without the basis of an authentic lineage and transmission. These teachers generally mix together elements from different spiritual and psychological traditions and then present them as their own original teachings. While studying with these kind of teachers may be pleasurable and create a sense of well-being and peace, at best this can only provide provisional benefits. At worst it can create a lot of obstacles. Here the real danger is that the energy of a pure teaching is diluted by being mixed with other approaches and is therefore misrepresented and taught without due authority.

According to Chögyal Namkhai Norbu, mixing the Dzogchen or Tantric teachings with a psychological discipline implies that the pure teaching or teacher is not perfect. The teachings themselves come from enlightened beings and do not need to be modified. New Age teachings can be enjoyable and in some ways helpful, but are not a vehicle for realization.

THE IMPORTANCE OF TRANSMISSION

Transmission is the link with the light of realization and the lineage of realized beings. To connect with this, we need a teacher who, in a very real sense, plugs us into the electrical current which is made active through their connection. Without this, it is very difficult to be connected to the lineage of realized beings. Sometimes it can happen through dreams or visions, but generally it is through physical contact with the teacher.

'If we have to light a lamp, we have to link up in some way with the current. When we've switched on or plugged in the current, then the lamp lights up. Transmission is similar.' [6]

Another example given is that of a blind person who is looking around in the dark for a valuable object. His only help is a friend who can see. The valuable object is the teachings, the friend is the teacher and we are the blind person, lost in the dark.

The process of connecting with the lineage of transmission goes back directly to Buddha Sakyamuni, and even earlier, through the generations to the original source of enlightenment. The teachers in this direct line of transmission are poetically described as being 'like high-tension electric wires strung across pylons spanning the countryside, bringing electric power to many distant cities from a single hydroelectric generating plant ...'[7]

The source of the transmission is always the teacher. The teacher is the source of knowledge, the door to the great stream of realization that has poured down through the centuries from one realized being to the next. It is always passed on with the intention that whoever is a suitable vessel for these precious teachings will also become realized, sooner or later. It is an extraordinary and awesome process, which has as its certainty all those men and women who have trod the same path before, whether it be 40 years before or 400 years, and who have achieved realization, freedom from the endless cycle of suffering. The path is the same, the realization is the same, but in our link with the lineage, we are beyond the normal constraints of time and space or distance. Without the teacher, though, there is no link to this precious inheritance.

'The sun is immensely powerful but to set fire to a piece of wood, it's more useful to have a magnifying glass that catches and intensifies the sunlight because the sun beaming down directly doesn't set fire to the wood.'[8]

'Therefore to start a fire, which is more important, the lens or the sun? Specifically to start a fire, the lens is.'[9]

There is a famous story of Padmasambhava and his consort Yeshe Tsogyal. Padmasambhava, while transmitting an initiation of Vajra Kilaya[fn2] to his disciples, manifested a divine *mandala* in front of his disciples. Out of profound respect, all his disciples but one paid homage to the miraculous *mandala*. Yeshe Tsogyal was the exception. She paid homage instead to her master, Padmasambhava, for she knew that without him, there would be no manifestation, no deity, no *mandala*: he alone was the source of all magical manifestation.

THREE KINDS OF TRANSMISSION

Dzogchen is a short and swift path which depends completely on the transmission from the teacher. There are three types of transmission – direct, symbolic and oral – which relate to the three dimensions or bodies of the Buddha, *dharmakaya*, *sambogakaya* and *nirmanakaya* (*see Chapter 3*).

Direct Transmission

Direct transmission comes straight from the teacher to the student through the union of the state of knowledge. It is considered that this knowledge came down directly from Samantabhadra to the five Buddha families.[fn3]

Frequently, direct transmission takes place in a most unorthodox way. With Tilopa and Naropa, Naropa was awakened by being slapped on the face with a wet fish. Patrul Rinpoche, the much-loved Tibetan vagabond saint of the nineteenth century, was awakened by his master Do Khyentse, whom he took to be a drunk! Do Khyentse, guessing his thoughts, spat in his face. Insulting him, he showed him his little finger and called him an Old Dog. At that point total clear realization of the luminous state of intrinsic awareness dawned in Patrul Rinpoche's mind: his mind and the non-dual mind of his master, the Buddha's mind, were completely merged.

One of the greatest lamas in eastern Tibet, Jamyang Khyentse, chose an outrageous way to awaken a proud young incarnate lama, the tulku Neten Choling Rinpoche, who was preparing to go to Lhasa for a debate with learned lamas. Before he left he attended a Tantric empowerment given by Jamyang Khyentse. The young Choling Tulku had very bad stomach cramps during the initiation and as Jamyang Khyentse came to bless his head with the golden initiation vase, '... to everyone's amazement, he kicked Neten

Choling in the guts. Choling had so much gas in his terribly upset stomach that he suddenly gave forth a magnificent, loud fart – hardly the thing to do in a temple, much less in such spiritual company.' [10] He was totally overcome with embarrassment when Khyentse Rinpoche shouted at him, 'That's it!' At that moment he was awakened and 'recognized the fundamental nature of being'.[11] He did not go to Lhasa for the debate. There was no need.

Symbolic Transmission

Symbolic transmission means that the transmission is done in a wordless fashion or without direct explanation. Generally it is done through a crystal, a mirror or even a peacock feather. Both the mirror and the crystal are symbols of the primordially pure state of mind, able to manifest infinite reflections without changing their own intrinsic pure nature. A peacock feather is a natural manifestation of infinite potentiality, symbolized through a circle or *thigle*[fn4] of five colours.

This type of transmission came from Vajrasattva[fn5], who exists in the dimension of light. *Vajra* means 'the primordial state of enlightenment' and *sattva* means 'a great being with this knowledge'. Vajrasattva's emanation in the human world was Garab Dorje, with whom the Dzogchen teachings originated on the human level.

Oral Transmission

Oral transmission takes place when the teachings are explained orally by the teacher so that the student can understand their primordial and perfected state of mind. It also includes methods of practice which are taught to enable the experience of this state of knowledge. Oral transmission originally came from Garab Dorje. He then taught Manjusrimitra, who was his first student (*see Chapter 7*).

These three transmissions are not just a question of historical understanding and, although categorized separately for the purposes of understanding, are not seen as fundamentally distinct. In other words the transmissions from the three dimensions of being, *dharmakaya*, *sambogakaya* and *nirmanakaya*, come from Samantabhadra, Vajrasattva and Garab Dorje. The three dimensions or *kayas* represent the body, voice and mind of the individual and are always present in any Dzogchen transmission, whatever form it takes. These three transmissions always exist in the teacher and therefore are always transmitted, whatever outer form is used.

It is important to recognize that transmission is an alive and continuous process and not just a question of relating to conceptual ideas about Samantabhadra or Vajrasattva, although it is useful to understand the origins of the state of knowledge. Today transmission to ordinary human beings predominantly takes place on an oral or spoken level, as most of our understanding comes through the intellect, although all three transmissions exist simultaneously.

'*My master gave me to understand that the presence of these three transmissions is not merely a matter of history, but rather that these transmissions must happen now when a master is transmitting right now, transmitting to a disciple. He is transmitting all three of these transmissions.*'[12]

Before transmission can take place, however, the master has to have knowledge of the enlightened state and know how to transmit it. Equally, the student must have the understanding and capacity for the transmission to be effective. One should not be fooled by lamas who just perform a lot of rituals but cannot give real transmission.

LONG AND SHORT TRANSMISSION LINEAGES

The teachings of Dzogchen are transmitted through two different kinds of lineage: *terma* and *kama*.

Terma

The *terma* teachings are called 'short and direct' (*nyegu*[fn6]). They are teachings which were hidden by Padmasambhava and his chief Tibetan consort, Yeshe Tsogyal, in the eighth–ninth century for rediscovery by later generations of visionary realized adepts, original disciples of Padmasambhava known as 'treasure finders' or *tertons*, i.e. those who discover treasure, or *terma*.

The 'short' lineage refers to the fact that there is only one teacher between oneself and the source of the teachings, Padmasambhava. This is the teacher who discovers the *terma*, who is then considered second in the lineage to Padmasambhava. That teacher is the *terton* who passes on these precious and powerful teachings to us, the students.

What is utterly marvellous is that this is not just historical fact, but is happening here and now in Britain, Europe, America – all around the globe wherever *tertons* are able to teach and transmit their precious and freshly revealed knowledge (*see Chapter 9*). Sometimes the *terma* may be only a couple of years old when they are transmitted to students. In other words, they are teachings only just revealed, and therefore they have an immediacy and relevance which renders them extremely potent. It is like eating bread hot out of the oven!

'The terma *teachings of the short and direct lineage are like the warm, fresh breath of the dakinis,*[fn7] *from which the moisture of blessings have not yet evaporated.*'[13]

Kama

Kama refers to the long lineage of teachings and transmissions which are passed down over the centuries from teacher to disciple in a slow and steady stream and are hundreds of years old.

The *kama* lineage is like a continuous chain of light. It encompasses the vast range of the teachings, and ensures the complete and full transmission of the body of teachings.

Ratna Lingpa (1403–1479) ensured the continuation of the *kama* tradition and its survival to this day. Furthermore, he was an important *terton* when the *kama* transmission of the Nyingmapa lineage was in critical danger of being lost, as copies of these texts were considered secret and were very rare.

Both lineages are important to practise, although realization can be gained by practising one alone. It is said that the complete fruit of the path can be gained by practising one *terma*, but that both lineages are needed to 'uphold all the teachings of the Buddhadharma in their totality'.[14]

It is not easy to find Dzogchen masters who are willing or able to transmit both *terma* and *kama* teachings. *Terma* teachings on their own, although profound and potent, do not ensure the full continuation of the three transmissions of the Dzogchen teachings: *Semde*, *Longde* and *Upadesha* (*see Chapter 3*). For this, the long *kama* lineage is required, from early historical times right up to the present day.

The source and lineage of the teachings presents a rich historical study impossible to cover in full, but short biographies of some outstanding masters of the Dzogchen lineage are detailed in the following chapters.

FOOTNOTES

fn1 *Lankavatara Sutra,* a Mahayana sutra which is very influential in both the Zen and Cittamatra (Mind Only) schools. It was translated into Tibetan from Chinese by the translator 'Gos Chos 'grub.

fn2 Vajrakilaya (Skt) (Tib. *rdo rje phur ba*) One of eight cycles of Tantric deities introduced to Tibet by Padmasambhava.

fn3 The five Buddha families represent the five aspects inherent in every individual relating to different passions and elements. The five families are Buddha, Vajra, Ratna, Padma and Karma.

fn4 *Thigle* (*thig.le*): Circle or tiny sphere (lit. 'drop') of light.

fn5 Vajrasattva (Skt) (Tib. *rdo rje sems dpa'*) *Vajra* means the primordial state of enlightenment. *Sattva* means a great being with this knowledge. Vajrasattva is white in colour and the practice of Vajrasattva is especially important for purification.

fn6 Nyegu (*nye brgyud*): Short and direct oral teachings in a few lines.

fn7 Dakini (*mkha' 'gro ma*): A feminine manifestation of enlightened energy, although some dakinis are also worldly.

CHAPTER 7

EARLY DZOGCHEN MASTERS

'The nature of the mind is Buddha from the
   beginning.
Mind, like space, has no birth or cessation.
Having perfectly realized the meaning of the oneness
   of all phenomena,
to remain in it, without seeking, is the meditation.'[1]

In terms of early Buddhist history, Dzogchen is said to have originated with Garab Dorje in Oddiyana 300 or 360 years after the *parinirvana* of Buddha Sakyamuni, although the exact date is in dispute. Many scholars associate Oddiyana with the Swat Valley in northern Pakistan, but it could also have been in Afghanistan.

Prior to this, though, some essential Dzogchen teachings had been transmitted through Shenrab Miwoche, the founder of the Bonpo,[fn1] the pre-Buddhist religion of Tibet. Other sources speak of much earlier teachers of Dzogchen, some of whom predate Garab Dorje by many thousands of years. The last of these teachers before Garab Dorje was Sakyamuni Buddha. These profound teachings are, therefore, by all accounts, extremely ancient. Furthermore, according to a Dzogchen *Upadesha* Tantra,

Tantra of the All-Surpassing Sound (Dra Thalgyur), they are also said to exist in at least 13 inhabited dimensions or solar systems beyond our own.

Imaginatively, this is where we enter an allegorical realm, where miracles occur. In the following stories of great Dzogchen adepts, normal reality is suspended, yet these accounts are documented and part of the historical and spiritual reality of the Dzogchen tradition.

GARAB DORJE, THE FIRST DZOGCHEN MASTER

Garab Dorje (*Prahevajra*) was born approximately 300 or 360 years after the *parinirvana* of Buddha Sakyamuni, although there is no exact date available for his birth and scholars differ in their opinions. He is considered to be the first human Knowledge Holder, *Rigdzin* or *Vidyadhara*, of the Dzogchen teachings in our world.

Garab Dorje had a miraculous birth. His mother was the Princess Sudharma, daughter of King Uparaja and Queen Alokabhashvati of Oddiyana. She had great compassion and virtue. A nun with a retinue of 500 other nuns, she kept her vows immaculately. One day she had a vision in which all the Buddhas sent rays of light which transformed into a sun and moon and entered her through the crown of her head and soles of her feet. The following day, Vajrapani[fn2], the Lord of Secrets, in the form of a swan, touched her three times on the heart with his beak. Then in the form of the seed syllable, HUM, representing the mind of all the Buddhas, he melted into her. Although she showed no signs of pregnancy, after nine months had passed, miraculously 'a gleaming nine-pointed *vajra* sprang from her heart. It then vanished, leaving in its place a child bearing the major and minor marks of Buddhahood, holding a *vajra* in his right hand and a rod of precious material in his left hand. He was reciting the lines beginning "Vajrasattva, vast as the sky [from *The Total Space of Vajrasattva*] ..."' [2]

Being a virgin, Princess Sudharma was ashamed of having given birth. Fearing that her child might be an evil spirit, she hid him in a pit of ashes, but sounds and lights came from the pit. After three days, she returned to find her child so shining and radiant that she burst into tears! Realizing that he must be a special being as he was still alive, she washed him with milk and water and wrapped him in white silk. She then brought him publicly to the palace. Here he was examined carefully by a Brahmin who proclaimed him to be one who 'would hold the teachings of the highest vehicle'. [3]

Considered an emanation of Vajrasattva, the child was named Garab Dorje, or 'Joyous Vajra', by his grandfather because everyone experienced such great joy in his presence. As he had arisen from a heap of ashes, he was also known as Ro lang Dewa, 'the Happy Zombie'.

Later Vajrapani appeared to him in a vision and conferred on him all the Tantras and pith (or essential) instructions of Dzogchen. Garab Dorje realized them all and effortlessly, in a single instant, attained Buddhahood. Although only seven years old, he begged his mother to let him go and debate with learned scholars. His mother had her doubts, 'Son, you haven't even lost your baby teeth. How can you discuss Dharma?' [4] But he persisted in his wish and went on to defeat with ease 500 learned scholars who had come from India especially to challenge him with their logic.

Garab Dorje taught 'the ultimate meaning of the Buddha's teachings ... centred on the recognition of the true nature of existence beyond the principle of cause and effect, only attainable by means of the path free of effort characteristic of Dzogchen *Atiyoga*.[5] After realizing all the root Tantras of Dzogchen, he began to teach Dzogchen to a few disciples. Then after spending 32 years in solitary retreat, he transmitted the Dzogchen teachings to a large number of dakinis as well as human disciples in the Shitavana cemetery and manifested in a number of miraculous ways through light. His chief disciple was Manjusrimitra, whom he taught for 75 years.

Garab Dorje passed away by dissolving his body into a vast cloud of brilliant rainbow light, accompanied by earth tremors and miraculous sounds. In despair Manjusrimitra called out to his beloved teacher, 'If the light that is our teacher is extinguished, who will be there to dispel the darkness of the world?'[6] At that moment Garab Dorje's right hand appeared, holding a golden casket making terrifying sounds, which then encircled Manjusrimitra three times before landing in his right palm. Inside this casket was 'a pressed seal of liquid lapis lazuli on a five-jewelled trumpet shell beating out'[7] the importance of Garab Dorje's final testament, *Hitting the Essence in Three Statements (Tsig sum ned dag)*, which is considered the essence of the Dzogchen teachings. Seeing this, Manjusrimitra immediately gained the same realization as Garab Dorje, his mind completely merged with the wisdom mind of his teacher.

MANJUSRIMITRA, THE MONK-SCHOLAR

Manjusrimitra was born to a Brahmin family who lived west of Bodhgaya in India. He became a monk-scholar and received a pure vision from Manjushri[fn3] instructing him to go to Oddiyana to meet Garab Dorje and request teachings to attain enlightenment in one lifetime:

'*Go to him and request the marvellous essence of the teachings, the Dharma known as* Atiyoga *which he holds, and through which Buddhahood can be attained without effort. You should be the compiler of his teaching.*'[8]

Despite this, Manjusrimitra travelled with six other scholars, not with a view of requesting the supreme teachings but arrogantly, intending to defeat Garab Dorje with logic. Yet, however hard they debated, they were unable to defeat him. To request teachings of Garab Dorje now seemed completely inappropriate and Manjusrimitra felt such intense remorse that in desperation he wanted to cut out his own tongue! He started looking for a razor, but Garab Dorje read his mind:

'*You will never purify your evil actions by cutting off your tongue! Compose a teaching far surpassing those dependent on the principle of cause and effect. That will purify you.*'[9]

The other scholars returned to India, feeling that they were unworthy of receiving teachings from Garab Dorje. Only Manjusrimitra had the excellent good fortune to remain and be able to absorb instantaneously all the profound teachings from his master. As penance for his arrogance and misdeeds, he wrote *The Bodhicitta of Pure Gold* and made a compilation of the teachings of Garab Dorje. He remained with Garab Dorje for 75 years and received the full transmissions of the complete Dzogchen lineage, as well as other *dharma* teachings.

It was Manjusrimitra who systematized the Dzogchen teachings into the Mind Series, *Semde*, the Series of Space, *Longde*, and the Essential *Upadesha* Instructions, classifications which are still used today (*see Chapter 3*). The Essential *Upadesha* Instructions he concealed north-east of Bodhgaya under a boulder sealed with a crossed *vajra*. Lighting a fire, he made it invisible until an auspicious time for their transmission.

It is said that he subsequently lived for 109 years at the Sosadvipa charnel ground, west of Bodhgaya, giving teachings to ugly dakinis, animals and Tantric practitioners. Amongst all the practitioners, he sat 'upon a throne supported by lions, and held upright various victorious standards which supported parasols of gold, silver and peacock feathers. Living in his multi-storied cemetery house, he was surrounded by a group of dakinis. For one hundred and nine years he stayed peacefully in meditation.'[10] It was here that he transmitted the Dzogchen teachings to Sri Singha, who in turn transmitted them to Padmasambhava, Jnanasutra, Vimalamitra and Vairocana.

At the end of his life, Manjusrimitra's body dissolved into rainbow light at the top of a *stupa* in the charnel ground of Sosadvipa.

He miraculously appeared again 325 years later in the west of India and became known as the Later Manjusrimitra. He taught both Padmasambhava and Aryadeva.

SRI SINGHA, JNANASUTRA AND VIMALAMITRA

Sri Singha stayed with Manjusrimitra as his disciple for 25 years. Once Manjusrimitra was sure of Sri Singha's understanding, he dissolved into rainbow light. From the sky he appeared and passed his last testament to Sri Singha in a casket of precious jewels the size of a fingernail. Written on a leaf of five precious substances were the few lines relating to *Upadesha* teachings, *The Six Experiences of Meditation*. The moment it touched his hand, Sri Singha understood the profound teachings and gained full realization.

Jnanasutra was a scholar who lived with 500 scholars in Bodhgaya. Amongst these was Vimalamitra, who subsequently became one of the greatest scholars in Tibet and with whom he had a close relationship from a previous life.

Sri Singha transmitted the first three cycles of the Essential Instructions to Vimalamitra and the complete four cycles to Jnanasutra. His last testament to Jnanasutra, as he dissolved into radiant rainbow light, was *The Seven Nails*, a summary of how to practise the *Upadesha* teachings.

In turn Jnanasutra transmitted these profound teachings and empowerments to his scholarly friend and companion Vimalamitra. Like Sri Singha, Jnanasutra's body disappeared into brilliant rainbow light, only to reappear to Vimalamitra in response to his anguished cries, dropping in his hand a casket of five precious stones, with the text *The Four Meditation Methods*, the Essential Instructions of *tregchod*. Vimalamitra immediately grasped their profound meaning.

Garab Dorje, toegether with Manjusrimtra, Sri Singha and Jnanasutra were the first four Knowledge Holders, *Rigdzin*, of the Dzogchen lineage in our human world. All of them left a testament to their heart disciples in exactly the same way, i.e. through a jewelled casket holding their last teachings. The minds of the disciples and the wisdom mind of the teachers were now inseparable.

PADMASAMBHAVA, THE GREAT GURU

The Great Guru, Padmasambhava, also known as the Second Buddha, was the master who firmly established the Tantric and Dzogchen teachings in Tibet in the ninth century AD. Like Sakyamuni Buddha, he was a fully realized being whose manifestation was predicted by the Buddha: 'After my nirvana ...

an individual greater than myself will appear on the lake isle of Dhanakosa.'[11]

There are two versions of his birth. The first and lesser known is that he was born as the son of the king of Oddiyana or one of his ministers. The more popular version is that he was born in a miraculous fashion from a lotus bud on an island in the Dhanakosha lake, Oddiyana, and is thus known as 'the Lotus-Born'. As an emanation of the Buddha Amitabha,[fn4] he arose from a golden *vajra*, marked with the seed syllable of Amitabha, *HRIH*, the syllable connected with long life and the western direction. Manifesting as a beautiful eight-year-old boy, adorned with all the marks of a Buddha, he stayed on the island teaching the dakinis and local gods. When the king of Oddiyana, Indrabhuti, met the miraculous child and asked him who he was, Padmasambhava sang:

> 'My father is the intrinsic awareness, Samantabhadra.
> My mother is the ultimate sphere, Samantabhadri.
> My lineage is the union of intrinsic awareness and
>   ultimate sphere.
> My name is the glorious Lotus-Born (Padmasam-
>   bhava).
> My country is the unborn ultimate sphere.
> I consume dualistic thoughts as food.
> My role is to accomplish the actions of the Buddhas.'[12]

Invited to Indrabhuti's palace to become his adopted son and crown prince, the Lotus-Born child, a true wish-fulfilling gem, satisfied all the needs of the population by raining food, clothing and precious jewels down on them. The kingdom, which had become bankrupt despite the king's boundless generosity, now prospered and happiness prevailed.

Destined to become king, Padmasambhava, like the Buddha before him, saw he had to renounce a public position in the kingdom to be of true spiritual service. By foreseeing the imminent death of an evil minister's son, he allowed his trident to fall and kill the boy. With great reluctance and sadness, King Indrabhuti was forced to banish Padmasambhava to wander in the charnel grounds. There he practised asceticism and the path of secret mantra amongst the dakinis, speaking to them in their symbolic language.

From Oddiyana, he travelled to India, where he studied all the Sutras and Tantras among learned masters. At Bodhgaya, he proclaimed that he was a self-realized Buddha but was insulted for this, despite performing miracles.

Free from the normal limitations of time and space, in Oddiyana he had received Dzogchen transmissions from Garab Dorje through a vision:

'He received empowerment from Ananda, a wisdom dakini in the form of a nun. She transformed Guru Rinpoche into a letter HUM, which she swallowed. In her body Guru Rinpoche was given the entire Outer, Inner and Esoteric empowerments, and she passed him out of her body through her padma.'[13]

In India he received further Dzogchen transmissions and teachings from Sri Singha, with whom he studied for 25 years, and from Manjusrimitra. In terms of Tantric practice, spontaneously, without any effort or concentrated meditational practice on deities, he beheld many divinities in pure vision.

Padmasambhava had two chief consorts, one an Indian princess, Mandarava, and the other a Tibetan princess, Yeshe Tsogyal. Popularly known as Guru Rinpoche, he travelled all over India and Nepal, bringing benefit to the people. There had been no rain in Nepal for three years and its people were afflicted by illness and hunger. By requesting specific texts of Vajrakila to be brought to Nepal, Guru Rinpoche overcame obstacles and reversed the fortunes of the country. There he practised with a Nepalese consort, Shakyadevi, the daughter of the king of Nepal.

His fame was such that King Trisong Detsen asked Guru Rinpoche to come to Tibet, on the advice of the teacher Shantarakshita, who had come from India to establish Buddhism in Tibet. Tibet was suffering famine, disease and drought. Hostile forces in the form of angry local spirits were plaguing the country-side, threatened by the attempt to introduce Buddhism into Tibet. The king, realizing that only Guru Rinpoche had the power to pacify these hostile spirits, sent gold to him and asked him to come to Tibet. Guru Rinpoche scattered the gold, proclaiming, 'Everything I perceive is gold.'[14] From then on Tibet became abundant in gold.

With his miraculous powers, Guru Rinpoche was able to travel all over Tibet, subduing the powerful non-human spirits and binding them with an oath to serve the Buddhist teachings. He brought 'all the spirits of Tibet under his command by dancing through the sky in fierce *vajra* steps',[15] thus subduing gods and demons and commanding them to help with the work of build-ing the temple of Samye:

> 'O gods and demons, build the temple!
> With humility and observance, all gather here to do
>   the work!
> Fulfil the wishes of Trisong Detsen!'[16]

This great temple was then built without any obstacles! It was con-structed in the image of Mount Sumeru. When Guru Rinpoche and Shantarakshita consecrated the monastery, extraordinary signs occurred: deities came to life and were seen outside the temple, accepting offerings of food as if they were people, flowers rained down to the sound of sacred music and rainbows filled the sky.

Many great Indian and Tibetan teachers and scholars resided at Samye, which was famous for its library, and translated Buddhist scriptures into Tibetan. Unsurpassed as a translator of Buddhist texts and one of Padmasambhava's closest disciples, Vairocana was the principal transmitter of two of the three series of Dzogchen teachings, viz. *Semde* and *Longde*.

Under the auspices of King Trisong Detsen, Buddhism was now firmly established by Padmasambhava, working together with Shantarakshita, Vimalamitra, Vairocana and other great scholars.

When the time came for Padmasambhava to leave Tibet and go to convert the ogres in the south-west, the king and ministers pleaded with him to stay. He responded:

> *'For devout people, Padmasambhava hasn't gone anywhere.*
> *For those who pray to me, I am always at their door ...'*[17]

Accompanied by the sound of divine music, he then flew off on a horse, or some say a lion, together with Yeshe Tsogyal, to the Copper-Coloured Mountain, his own pure realm. There he parted from his consort Yeshe Tsogyal, comforting her with the words:

'Contemplate in the essence of Dzogchen, effortlessly.
There are no teachings superior to this.
The love of Padmasambhava has no rising or setting
    but will always be there.
The link of light of my compassion for Tibet will never
    be severed even after I have departed.
For my children who pray to me, I am always in front
    of them.
For people who have faith, there is no separation
    from me.' [18]

Accounts vary as to the time that Guru Rinpoche stayed in Tibet. Some say he was there for a matter of months, others that he was there for as long as 54 or 55 years, but this is only a limited historical notion. His activity went far beyond the narrow constraints of time, with his capacity to manifest simultaneously in all Buddha fields as well as in different parts of Tibet at will. He is also able to manifest at will anywhere to those with pure devotion.

MANDARAVA, THE QUEEN OF LONG LIFE

Mandarava was an emanation of Pandaravasini, the consort of Amitabha, the Buddha of the Western Paradise. Her parents were the king and queen of Sahor, now known as Mandi, in Himachal Pradesh, northern India.

Auspicious visions of the five Buddhas, together with their consorts, heralded Mandarava entering her mother's womb, as well as an abundance of flowers and grain falling from the skies. When the baby girl was in her womb, the queen experienced great bliss, becoming more and more youthful with each month. At night her body became totally luminous. Having suffered no discomfort throughout her pregnancy, she gave birth painlessly amidst wondrous signs of rainbow light and sweet music. The girl child was radiant, chanting, 'OM, AH, HUM,' as well as the vowels and consonants of the alphabet. To her parents, she sang:

'I am the mother of the buddhas of the three times, the incarnate one known as Pandaravasini. There are millions of female bodhisattvas just like me who come into this world like rain pouring down.' [19]

After three months, a holy man declared her to be a wisdom dakini, destined to become the consort of a miraculously born prince.

When she was only eight years old, looking outside the palace walls, Mandarava felt deeply moved at the profound suffering she saw there. Weeping, she asked her mother if she could leave the palace and practise the *dharma*. As she was so young and beautiful, her parents could not allow her to leave but permitted her to stay in her own chambers in the palace and practise there. She studied deeply and wisely and became a great scholar by the time she was only 13 years old.

Her fame was such that it spread through all the neighbouring kingdoms and each kingdom wanted her as their queen. Her parents had to placate her royal suitors with wealth, but they would not be deterred. Mandarava had no choice now but to become a nun, formally renouncing the world and all her potential suitors! Her 500 servants were also ordained. A new palace was built for her near the king's palace and together with her nuns, she studied there and spent time in retreat.

At her ordination, it was predicted that she would become a disciple of Padmasambhava, the second Buddha. A dream presaged her meeting with him, on top of a grassy hill, as predicted. Mandarava, together with her assembly of nuns, experienced overwhelming devotion to the Great Guru. In her palace, he then transmitted the full range of secret mantra teachings. All seemed well until a cowherd, spying through a crack in a cave on the mountain, saw Padmasambhava and Mandarava in bliss-ful union and spread malicious gossip which eventually reached the king. Not understanding the nature of the relationship, he simply thought that a vagabond was consorting with his royal daughter and ordered him to be burned alive. He was almost equally harsh with his daughter and ordered:

'Throw her into a dark pit of thorns, where she shall remain for twenty-five human years without seeing the light of day. Place her two main attendants in darkness and the remaining five hundred servants in confinement! Make certain that they never even hear the sound of a male voice.' [20]

The pit still exists in Mandi to this day, suffused with an unmis-takable presence of deep serenity and spirituality. Guru Rinpoche transformed the fire into a lake of sesame seed oil and manifested on a lotus in the lake as an eight-year-old boy with all the marks of a Buddha. Horrified, the king realized that he had transgressed against a holy being and, stricken with profound remorse, offered him his kingdom and crown. Padmasambhava accepted the crown and boots of the king and was drawn to the palace in a car-riage pulled by the king himself, as penance.

Mandarava was distraught at the treatment of her consort and teacher and refused to return to the palace, even at her father's request. Finally she relented and returned, granting her father forgiveness, and was reunited, weeping, with Guru Rinpoche. The king offered the wealth of his kingdom to his daughter, and Guru Rinpoche became king of Zahor and gave teachings.

Mandarava then went with Guru Rinpoche to the cave of Maratika in Nepal, where together they gained the siddhi of Long Life from the Buddha of Infinite Life, Amitayus, and Mandarava gained the status of a pure Knowledge Holder, or *Vidyadhara*. To show her attainment of immortality, she is thus always depicted holding an arrow of long life with five coloured ribbons symbolizing the five elements.

Mandarava also travelled with Padmasambhava to Kotala and the great charnel grounds, subduing opposition by manifesting as the fierce lion-headed dakini Simhamukha and giving teachings. She then buried secret Dzogchen texts at Mount Kailash.

After travelling through Nepal, manifesting as a body of brilliant light in the sky and subduing evil butchers in India, she returned to her home of Zahor. Here she showed her parents her miraculous attainments: '[Opening] up her chest, she revealed to them the entire mandala within her heart, a pantheon of long-life deities, lucidly clear.'[21] Remaining in her family kingdom for one year, she taught continuously and during that period both her parents, the king and queen, were realized and the whole kingdom was liberated.

Both Mandarava and Padmasambhava then went to Oddiyana, remaining there for 13 years. Afterwards Padmasambhava sent Mandarava to Shambhala, where she performed various miracles such as bringing a corpse back to life, transforming dead soldiers' bodies into rainbow light and curing lepers with her own urine. She induced faith in all those who met her. In one city, she even manifested in countless forms and engaged in lovemaking with all the men there, thus liberating them. Burnt alive by the king of the northern continent, like Padmasambhava before her she manifested a lake on which she was seated in the centre on a lotus. Great faith arose throughout all Shambhala. In all it is said that hundreds of thousands of Mandarava's disciples in Shambhala gained realization.

At the end of her life, Mandarava dissolved into a mass of rainbow light, promising, 'As you abide in the equipoise of your own true nature, I, the consort Mandarava, will appear to you in symbolic visions. Pray to me and you shall encounter your own true face!' [22] As a body of light, Mandarava still appears to those who supplicate her with extreme devotion and her presence fills her small cave high up on the mountainside of Rewalsar, northern India.

YESHE TSOGYAL, THE TREASURE-HOLDER

Yeshe Tsogyal was considered an incarnation of Vajravarahi, the Sow-Headed Goddess, [fn5] and Tara. [fn6] At her conception, both parents had visions: her mother saw a golden bee and her father, Prince Pelgi Wangchuk, beheld an eight-year-old girl singing the vowels of the Sanskrit alphabet and the seed syllable *HRI*. Both parents felt their dreams foretold a marvellous event. Nine months later, her mother gave birth, without any pain, to the spontaneous manifestation of mantric sound and the recitations of Tantras. A spring by the royal castle turned into a lake, increasing in size at the birth. Consequently the baby was called Tsogyal, meaning 'Victorious Ocean'. The banks of the lake were covered in red and white flowers and the birth was heralded by rainbow light, melodious music and a rainfall of flowers.

Yeshe Tsogyal grew up an exceptional beauty, with many suitors wanting her hand. This led to strife in the kingdom, which was finally resolved by King Trisong Detsen asking to marry her, to which she agreed. Later she became the consort to Guru

Rinpoche, given as a precious offering by the king in exchange for teachings and empowerments. She received nearly all Guru Rinpoche's teachings and was so purely devoted to him that she gained realization: 'All his knowledge became hers, as if the water from one vessel was poured into another.' [23] Through the blessing of the Goddess of Learning, Saraswati, she had the most extraordinary memory and was able to write down all the teachings of Padmasambhava, concealing many hidden treasures, *terma*, to be rediscovered at a later date (*see Chapter 9*). After Guru Rinpoche left Tibet, she stayed on for another 200 years, concealing *terma* treasures and bringing hundreds of people to realization:

'Her body, purified and transformed through yogic mastery, was a supreme vajra *body, radiant with the vitality of youth, and looking like that of a beautiful sixteen-year-old girl. On one occasion when seven lustful men were raping her, she seized the opportunity to liberate them ... When a leper, his body decomposing, spewing with blood and pus and reeking of decay, asked her to be his woman, she served him. She gave her body to wild animals, she gave clothing to those who were cold, food to the hungry, medicine to the sick, protection to the powerless.'* [24]

When Yeshe Tsogyal was 190 years old, she met Mandarava, the Indian consort of Padmasambhava, and requested from her the teachings on long life which she had not received from Guru Rinpoche.

At the end of her life, she took her leave: 'This wild lady has done everything ... has shaken things up far and wide ... I will take my winding way into the expanse of the *dharma*. I have not died, I have not gone anywhere.' [25] Her body dissolved into light and she left for the Copper-Coloured Mountain, the pure realm of Guru Rinpoche, to be reunited with her consort.

The Buddha in the Deer Park at Sarnath, where he gave his first teachings

The Dharmakaya Buddhas, Samantabhadra in union with Samantabhadri (painting by Dolma Beresford)

His Holiness the fourteenth Dalai Lama

Dilgo Khyentse as a young man in Tibet

Milarepa, the eleventh-
century yogi and poet
*(Hemis Monastery,
Ladakh)*

Earth Terma image of
Guru Rinpoche (*ku tsab*
or representative figure),
clay figurine

Machig Labdron, the female Chöd master *(collection of Chögyal Namkhai Norbu)*

Statue of Tara, female
deity of compassion
*(collection of Chögyal
Namkhai Norbu)*

The contemporary Dzogchen master, Chögyal Namkhai Norbu, with
vajra and bell *(Italy, 1980)*

His Holiness Dudjom
Rinpoche, the renowned
Nyingma master

Garab Dorje, the first human Dzogchen
Master (painting by Glen Eddy)

Gomadevi, an important Dzogchen female master and
the source of the Vajra Dance *(painting by Dugu Chögyal
Rinpoche at Merigar, Italy)*

FOOTNOTES

[fn1] Bonpo: The most common religion in Tibet before Buddhism arrived in the ninth century. Bonpos claim that Shenrab Miwoche, the great Bon master, was the first person to teach Dzogchen in Central Asia more than 3,800 years ago, but there is no written proof of this. He taught 12 Dzogchen Tantras in a very abbreviated form: the Twelve Small Tantras (*rGyud bu chung bcu gnyis*).

[fn2] Vajrapani (*phyag na rdo rje*), one of the three main deities in Kriyatantra, one of the eight main Bodhisattvas, manifests in either a peaceful or wrathful form. He is the chief compiler of Vajrayana teachings and is also known as the Lord of Secrets. Mahamudra transmission comes through Vajrapani.

[fn3] Manjushri is the Bodhisattva of Wisdom.

[fn4] Amitabha: Red Buddha of the western direction.

[fn5] Vajravarahi (*rdo rje phag mo*) is a very important dakini, very close in manifestation to Vajrayogini. She is known as the 'Vajra Sow' as she is depicted with a sow's head over her right ear.

[fn6] Tara (Skt) (Tib. *sgrol ma*): A female Buddha of Compassion known as the 'Mother of all the Buddhas'. Her image is found throughout Tibet in all the schools. Usually depicted as green in colour, she acts swiftly for the benefit of all beings when requested. She has 21 different manifestations. One of the best known is White Tara, who is associated with long life. She is accorded great devotion by both Tibetans and Western practitioners.

CHAPTER 8

LATER LINEAGE OF KNOWLEDGE

'The nature of the mind is like openness, space.
But it is superior, as it possesses the wisdom.
Luminous clarity is like the sun and moon,
But it is superior, as there are no substances.
Intrinsic awareness is like a crystal ball,
But it is superior, as there are no obstructions or
coverings.'[1]

LONGCHENPA, THE GREAT SCHOLAR
(1308–1363)

Longchenpa was one of the greatest scholars and most highly realized masters in Tibet. When he was conceived his mother dreamed of a huge lion whose forehead, completely lit up by the rays of the sun, illuminated the three worlds of existence.[fn1] He was considered an incarnation of a daughter of King Trisong Detsen and at an early age showed all the qualities of a Bodhisattva: rich in learning and wisdom, he was full of compassion and faith. By the time he was 19, he was known as a brilliant scholar and became known as Longchen Rabjampa, 'The Extensively Learned One who is Like Vast Space'.[2] Devoted to meditation practice, he had pure visions of a number of deities, including Manjusri, Sarasvati, Vajravarahi and Tara. It is said that Sarasvati, the Goddess of Powerful Speech, carried him in the palm of her hand for seven days and prophesied his enlightenment.

Disillusioned with worldly suffering and the behaviour of fellow Khampa scholars, Longchenpa chose the life of a wandering practitioner. At 28, as predicted by Tara, he met his root teacher, the Rigdzin Kumaradza. Kumaradza had dreamed of his arrival:

'Last night I dreamt that a wonderful bird, which announced itself to be a divine bird, came with a large flock in attendance, and carried away my books in all directions. Therefore, someone will come to hold my lineage.'[3]

Longchenpa stayed with Kumaradza for two years, wandering constantly amidst great hardship and discomfort, sometimes in freezing conditions and for periods living only on the tiniest amount of flour and some long-life pills. Such were his austere conditions that he lived in a sack which he used both as a robe and to sleep in! During this period, however, he received teachings on all three categories of Dzogchen, including Vimalamitra's *Nyingthig* transmission, and was declared to be Kumaradza's successor.

For about seven years Longchenpa was in retreat in mountainous caves, mainly at Chimphu, and had visions of Padmasambhava, Vajrasattva, Guru Dragpo[fn2] and countless other Buddhas and Bodhisattvas. Vimalamitra appeared in a vision, empowering him to teach from his own transmission, the *Vima Nyingthig*[fn3]. Longchenpa also wrote commentaries on the *Khandro Nyingthig*[fn4] and *Vima Nyingthig*. He restored the temple at Samye, finding a chest of gold under the shrine to fund the work. The Dzogchen protector, Dorje Legpa,[fn5] appearing as a boy with a turquoise earring, helped with the reconstruction, working every day with the builders.

Longchenpa always lived in the utmost simplicity and praised the life of solitude:

> '*Far from the towns full of entertainments,*
> *Being in the forests naturally increases the peaceful*
>   *absorptions,*
> *Harmonizes life in* Dharma, *tames the mind,*
> *And makes one attain ultimate joy.*'[4]

Never taking money for himself, he was always generous and kind to the poor and gave away any offerings to further the teachings. He left behind more than 250 bodies of work, including the *Seven Treasures*. Most of his works on Dzogchen and Tantra are considered to be Mind Treasures (*see Chapter 9*).

At the end of his life, his body was left undisturbed for 25 days, protected by a tent of rainbow light. Although it was the middle of winter, ice melted and flowers bloomed. At his cremation, the earth trembled and in the sky loud thunder was heard seven times. Five large relics or *dungsel*[fn6], pearl-like relics, were left in the ashes, showing his realization of the five bodies of Buddhahood, as well as numerous small relics or *ringsel*, tiny sacred relic pills.

LONGCHENPA'S VISIONARY DISCIPLE: JIGME LINGPA (1730–1798)

Jigme Lingpa was considered the emanation of both Vimalamitra and King Trisong Detsen. He had a simple upbringing, free from any pomp, even though both his parents came from well-known families, and retained this simplicity throughout his life. From birth, his body carried auspicious signs. His heart was studded with small moles in the shape of a *vajra* and his navel had them in the shape of a bell; on his right thumb was the syllable *HRI* and one of his teeth was marked with the syllable *AH*, a sign of being the reincarnation of Vimalamitra.

As a young novice monk, he was more interested in playing than studying, but he did show intense compassion for all living beings, especially animals. He was able to absorb learning simply by listening to other students or just seeing texts. At 13 he met his root guru, Rigdzin Thugchok Dorje, who was a great *terton*. He studied under a number of other masters, but always concentrated on essential teachings. From the age of 27, he spent three years in retreat in a hermitage at Pelri monastery. In visions he received blessings directly from Guru Rinpoche, Yeshe Tsogyal and Manjusrimitra, amongst others. Having attained yogic mastery of all his channels and chakras, he 'perceived all appearances as a book and the great treasury of the doctrine spilled open in the form of songs of indestructible reality and so forth, which were perfect in word and meaning'.[5] From then on, he grew his hair long and wore the plain white robes of a yogi instead of the maroon robes of a monk.

At 28, he was entrusted the Mind *terma* of the *Longchen Nyingthig* cycle by a wisdom dakini at Bodhnath *stupa* in Nepal, to which he had travelled in a state of meditative absorption. The wisdom dakini gave him a wooden casket:

'*[With]an experience of great joy, he opened the casket. In it he found five rolls of yellow scrolls with seven crystal beads. At first, the script was illegible, but then it turned into Tibetan script. One of the rolls was ...* Nechang Thukkyi Drombu, *the prophetic guide of* Longchen Nyingthig[fn7]. *Rahula, one of the protectors of the teachings, appeared before him to pay respect. As he was encouraged by another dakini, Jigme Lingpa swallowed all the yellow scrolls and the crystal beads. Instantly, he had the amazing experience that all the words of the* Longchen Nyingthig *cycle with their meanings had been awakened in his mind as if they were imprinted there.*'[6]

Jigme Lingpa thus attained realization as a *terton*. He kept these teachings secret for seven years. Thereafter he went again into retreat in the caves at Chimphu, near Samye. There he had three visions of Longchenpa, in which he received the full transmission and blessings of Longchenpa's body, speech and mind, now fully empowering him to transmit the *Longchen Nyingthig*.

When he came out of retreat, although much weakened physically through lack of food, he had a vision of Thangtong Gyalpo,[fn8] who possessed the power of longevity. Through this, he quickly regained his strength. Recognizing that the time was now auspicious and at the request of one of his clairvoyant disciples, he taught the *Longchen Nyingthig* first to 15 fortunate disciples at Samye and then more widely. These teachings of the *Longchen Nyingthig* are widespread today and still actively practised.

Living life as a simple yogi in the hermitage he had built at Tsering Jong (together with a meditation school), Jigme Lingpa transmitted Nyingma teachings, particularly Dzogchen, to all who came to him. Showing no interest in worldly ambitions like power or wealth, he continued to live an ascetic life with the minimum of needs. In his two testaments, one included this verse:

'I am always in the state of ultimate nature;
For me there is not staying or going.
The display of birth and death is mere relativity.
I am enlightened in the great primordial liberation![7]

Following his childhood love for animals, he saved many animals from hunters or butchers. He reconsecrated Samye and was able to repel a Gurkha army hostile to the teachings by means of ritual practices. He had copies made, in 25 volumes, of the precious texts of the Nyingmapa which had been found at Mindroling, and composed *The History of the Nyingma Tantras*, elucidating his own now brilliant scholarship. His works are found in nine volumes, including the famous *Yeshe Lama*, which is extensively used by practitioners today.

At the age of 65, Jigme Lingpa and his consort had a son who was recognized as the reincarnation of Chokyi Nyima, one of the two heads of the Drigung Kagyu tradition.[fn9] Travelling with his son to his enthronement four years later, Jigme Lingpa, now old and frail, fell seriously ill, but recovered after taking a long-life pill. At the age of 70, he warned a close disciple that he would die soon. After he gave a teaching on White Tara, the Tara of Long Life, his hermitage became filled with sweet-smelling fragrance. Although the sky was clear, rain fell lightly, and at night, sitting upright, he died. Relics appeared from his teeth and hair. His body was kept in a small *stupa* at Tsering Jong hermitage, which became a nunnery and was destroyed only in the last 25 years.

A subsequent incarnation of Jigme Lingpa was Jamyang Khyentse Wangpo, who lived in the nineteenth century (*see page 128*). Born amidst wondrous signs, he was undoubtedly one of the most important masters in promoting an open and non-sectarian approach to Tibetan Buddhism which is still influential today and is known as Rime, which means having an unbiased respect for all traditions.

PATRUL RINPOCHE, THE ENLIGHTENED VAGABOND (1808–1887)

A much-loved vagabond and master, Patrul Rinpoche was recognized as the speech incarnation of Jigme Lingpa. At his birth in Kham, eastern Tibet, his neck was inscribed with *OM MANI PADME HUM*, the mantra of the Buddha of Compassion, Avalokitesvara, and only a few days after his birth he was heard chanting the mantra clearly.

Despite being an important incarnation and a great scholar and master, Patrul Rinpoche lived one of the most humble and simple lives, disclaiming wealth and possessions. His main teachers were Jigme Gyalwai Nyugu (Jigme Lingpa's chief disciple) and Do Khyentse, a fiery and crazy yogi.

From Jigme Gyalwai Nyugu, Patrul Rinpoche received the *tsalung*[fn10] teachings of Jigme Lingpa and at least 14 times the preliminary practices of the *Longchen Nyingthig*. He wrote down his teacher's commentary on these preliminary practices in the famous text *The Words of My Perfect Teacher (Kunzang Lama'i Shelung)*, which is widely studied today. Jigme Gyalwai Nyugu also gave him teachings on Dzogchen.

Patrul Rinpoche transmitted the two lineages of *tsalung* and *Yeshe Lama* to Adzam Drugpa (*see page 110*) in return for a favour: Adzam Drugpa had helped his mother at death, guiding her consciousness through the intermediate state, or *bardo* (*see Chapter 10*).

Through Do Khyentse, a completely unorthodox Dzogchen master, Patrul Rinpoche earned the nickname 'Old Dog' and subsequently referred to himself by this name: 'Thanks to Lord Khyentse's unique kindness, now my Dzogchen name is Old Dog. Wanting and needing nothing, I just wander freely round and round.'[8]

In fact Patrul Rinpoche lived the life of a beggar, wandering round the countryside dressed as a nomad in an old ragged sheepskin coat and sleeping wherever he found himself. He refused offerings of gold and silver, finding them too much trouble! He was more concerned with the essence of the teachings and bringing Buddhism into everyday life. He discouraged the offering of meat to lamas and forbade hunting and stealing, sometimes reforming hunters and robbers just by his very presence. In some areas, he inspired the whole population to recite the mantra of compassion, *OM MANI PADME HUM*, and in his home territory of Dzachuka he spent many years adding stones to a wall, each of which was carved with this mantra. From then on he started accepting offerings such as butter, which he used to pay people to carve mantras on the stone wall.

For a long time he lived in seclusion under a tree in the Ari Forest. The only other inhabitant of the forest was Nyoshul Lungtok. They met every day under a tree at lunchtime, when they ate a little *tsampa* (Tibetan barley flour) together and Patrul Rinpoche gave Nyoshul Lungtok teachings on the *Bodhicharyavatara*, 'The Bodhisattva's Way of Life', by Shantideva. Before long, other disciples heard of this enlightened vagabond, living on almost nothing except a tiny bit of *tsampa*, and came to receive teachings. The forest did not provide edible vegetation, and tea was used and reused until it completely lost its colour and taste! But for Patrul Rinpoche, wealth only created problems:

'Poverty is good and prosperity is not good.
Prosperity causes the great pains of earning more and
preserving it.' [9]

At the age of 78, Patrul Rinpoche passed away into a state of absorption and remained in a state of contemplation beyond birth and death. He left nothing of any material value, only a set of robes, a bowl, shawl, a little food and six books. In life, he was simple, direct, compassionate and often rough in his manner, so as to awaken people. Everyone was treated as equal, from beggars to kings, and he was completely non-sectarian in his approach to the various schools of Tibetan Buddhism. Although he was what is known as a 'hidden yogi', he was described by the third Dodrupchen as pure gold: 'Even if the gold remains underground, its light radiates into the sky.' [10] He left behind writings in six volumes, including remarkably concise instructions on Dzogchen: *The Three Statements that Strike the Essence* and *The Words of My Perfect Teacher: Kunzang Lama'i Shelung*. Among his disciples were Lama Mipham and Ogyen Tendzin, the uncle of Chögyal Namkhai Norbu.

NYAGLA PADMA DUDDUL (1816–1872)

Born in Kham, Padma Duddul was a contemporary of Do Khyentse, Patrul Rinpoche and Adzam Drugpa. At birth he was named Tashi Tondrub and he grew up to be an extremely intelligent child. His father died when he was young and the family was left penniless. Forced out of their own house by an aunt, they had to live in the stable. Even their few animals were stolen from them, so life was very hard. Two of Tashi Tondrub's brothers died of starvation and he tried to eke out a living tending animals.

Fortunately his uncle, Rigdzin Drodul Osal Dorje, was a great *terton* and gave him a series of teachings on Tara, which he had discovered himself. Entrusted with these teachings, Tashi Tondrub:

'... *experienced a reawakening and he was suddenly able to do many things that he had previously been unable to do and that no one had taught him. He was spontaneously able to perform rituals and knew all the proper preparations connected to them. He knew how to play instruments, paint, and carve mantras on rocks. He also knew the crafts of metallurgy and carpentry. With all these abilities he was able to resolve his economic problems in a short time and secure a better life for his mother.*'[11]

At the age of 18, a dream of beings in the hell realms so deeply affected him that he prayed for their salvation and at that moment his uncle appeared in the form of Avalokitesvara, instructing him to do a certain practice which would enable him to help countless beings. At 21 he met Do Khyentse and received the *Longchen Nyingthig* teachings. When he was 25, he received further teachings on the *Longchen Nyingthig* from Padma Gyurme Sangye, who gave him the name Padma Duddul.

Padma Duddul was a great *terton*. He had frequent visions of Guru Rinpoche. At the age of 36 he received a list of *terma* that would come to him and one of the teachings he received was of Amitayus, the Buddha of Limitless Life.

He also received the essential Dzogchen teachings of *yangtig*, 'The Single Golden Syllable of the Black Quintessence', and did many retreats in the dark. In 1872, at the age of 56, he attained Rainbow Body (*see Chapter 11*). Although not well known in his lifetime, after achieving Rainbow Body, he became famous. He taught a number of male and female disciples, many of whom attained the same state of knowledge as he did, and was one of the main teachers of Changchub Dorje, Adzam Drugpa and Ayu Khandro amongst others.

ADZAM DRUGPA, THE *DRUGCHEN* OR GREAT DRAGON (1842–1924)

Adzam Drugpa, also known as Rigdzin Natsok Rangdrol, was one of the great Dzogchen masters of the last hundred years and one of the greatest exponents of the *Longchen Nyingthig* teachings, transmitting them 38 times. He received *Nyingthig tsa lung* practices and Jigme Lingpa's *Yeshe Lama* from Patrul Rinpoche, and was the only holder of these lineages.

Seven days after his birth he was heard reciting the six-syllable mantra of the Buddha of Compassion, Avalokitesvara, *OM MANI PADME HUM*. At only three years old, he declared himself to be an emanation of Pema Karpo, also known as the *Drugchen* or Great Dragon, a great scholar and master of the Drugpa Kagyud school. When he was nine years old, this was confirmed by many lamas, including the great Jamyang Khyentse Wangpo, and he began to have pure visions of Yeshe Tsogyal.

On the advice of Jamyang Khyentse Wangpo and Nyagla Padma Duddul, Adzam Drugpa became a Tantric practitioner and grew his hair long.

In an evocative song written by Lhundrub Tso, Chögyal Namkhai Norbu's grandmother, chronicling briefly Adzam Drugpa's life story, she wrote that his knowledge was completely awakened by the Direct Introduction (*rigpai tsal wang*) given by Padma Duddul. He saw both Jigme Lingpa and Longchenpa in visions and received teachings directly from them. He became an important *terton* and taught the great lamas of Dzogchen at Palyul, Kathok and Zhechen monasteries.

Many disciples, both Tibetan and Chinese, came to Adzamgar in eastern Tibet where he taught Dzogchen teachings principally for three months in the summer. In the winter he gave *tsa lung* practices.

'When we returned to Kham, my father, my eldest brother Shedrup, and myself [sic] met the great teacher Adzam Drugpa. He was a very impressive man. He wore a white raw silk shirt with a collar of red brocade and had a chain of onyx round his neck. He had long black hair with a touch of silver, tied up on top of his head with a scarf.'[12]

Adzam Drugpa dispelled an obstacle to Dilgo Khyentse's life by giving him a long-life blessing every day for seven days.

One of his chief disciples, and the first Dzogchen teacher of Chögyal Namkhai Norbu, was the yogi Togden Ogyen Tendzin, Chögyal Namkhai Norbu's paternal uncle, whose story is told elsewhere (*see Chapter 11*).

At the age of 83, Adzam Drugpa seated in contemplation, pronounced the syllable *HIK*, transferring his consciousness, and then remained seated in meditation for three weeks until his body shrank to the size of an eight year old. Thunder was heard and rainbows filled the sky, 'all of space was filled with rainbows ... among the flames were appearing *HUM* of five colours ... even the smoke took the form of *HUM*'.[13] Even his bones and ashes were brilliant with rainbow-coloured light and more than 3,000 tiny relics manifested from his body.

Chögyal Namkhai Norbu was recognized as his reincarnation when he was two years old, and later by the sixteenth Karmapa[fn11] and Situ Rinpoche[fn12] as the Shabdrung Rinpoche,[fn13] the Dharmaraja or ruler of Bhutan.

AYU KHANDRO, THE DAKINI OF GREAT BLISS (1839–1953)

Born on the day of the dakinis in 1839 amongst auspicious signs, Ayu Khandro was called Dechen Khandro, which means 'Dakini of Great Bliss'. She was a remarkable yogini who lived to be 115 years old, practising for more than 50 years in total darkness. Little known, she had very few students because she lived most of her life in retreat. She studied under Padma Duddul and Jamyang Khyentse Wangpo, but a strong influence on her early life was her aunt, who was a dedicated practitioner and was later recognized as a great yogini.

From early childhood, Ayu Khandro was interested in the teachings, and between the ages of 7 and 18 helped her aunt in retreat by bringing water and wood to her cave. During this period, she also received teachings and initiations from some great lamas, including Jamyang Khyentse Wangpo and Situ Rinpoche. From Nyagla Padma Duddul, she received the name Dorje Paldron, which means 'Glorious Indestructible *Vajra*'.

Despite her aunt's advice, her parents betrothed her while young to the scion of a wealthy family, Apho Wangdo. By the time she was 19, her family insisted on her marriage, although her aunt felt strongly that she should be allowed to continue with her religious practice.

After three years of marriage to Apho Wangdo, who was a good and kind man, Ayu Khandro fell ill with an undiagnosed condition, and in her own words,

'… *slowly weakened for two years. The sickness could not even be diagnosed. Sometimes it seemed like a prana[fn14] disease, at other times I had convulsions like epilepsy; sometimes it seemed like a circulation problem. In short none of the doctors could help or even distinguish what the problem was. Whatever ritual or medicine was advised had little effect. I became worse and worse and was near to death when they finally asked Togden Rangrig to come to see me.*[14]

Finally only a long-life initiation given by the Togden brought her back to life. Both the Togden and Ayu Khandro's aunt felt that the cause of this mysterious illness was her marriage, which was preventing her from fulfilling her spiritual potential. Fortunately her husband agreed to release her from her marriage commitments. They maintained a harmonious relationship and the following year he acted as her patron, making sure she had enough food supplies. Later, he built her a retreat hut.

After her aunt's death, Ayu Khandro did a three-year retreat in her cave. She then met Adzam Drugpa. Accompanied by her friend, Padma Yangkyi, she travelled around the countryside, doing the practice of Chöd in cemeteries and terrifying places in order to overcome fear and attachment to the body. Later, when they met Nyagla Padma Duddul, he gave them both a Chöd drum and prophesied that they would meet two yogis on their travels who would be helpful in their spiritual development. The first was Togden Semnyi, whom they heard singing beautifully in a cemetery. He gave them teachings on Chöd and they travelled together, doing practice. They met the second yogi in southern Tibet. His name was Togden Trulzhi and he was a disciple of a famous yogini, Mindroling Jetsun Rinpoche. As a group, they travelled together, practising Chöd extensively until their fame in Nepal became an obstacle and they left for Khyung Lung and Mount Kailash in western Tibet.

For a few years Ayu Khandro travelled extensively with Togden Semnyi, visiting sacred places and receiving teachings.

Then, setting off for the place where she had first married, she found the retreat centre in ruins and the cave of her aunt unrecognizable. A vision indicated she should go to a place where there was an 'egg-shaped rock in Dzongtsa, which I could enter through a cave. When I got inside there was a very intense darkness which suddenly was illuminated by multi-coloured light streaming out of it. This illuminated the cave and pierced the walls so that I could see through to the outside.'[15]

Arriving near Dzongtsa, Ayu Khandro found the place of her vision, but it was the other side of a river which was too high to cross. After practising for three days, in a dream she saw a long white bridge spanning the river, which she crossed in her dream state. The next morning, miraculously she was on the other side of the river. There she was able to stop an epidemic amongst the nomads' animals by practising Chöd.

As Ayu Khandro gained fame, she decided to become stricter in her retreat and her husband agreed to build her a retreat hut. After visiting Adzam Drugpa, Jamyang Khyentse Wangpo and Kongtrul Rinpoche and receiving further teachings, she went into retreat for seven years, until the death of Jamyang Khyentse Wangpo. Then she vowed to stay in retreat for the rest of her life and alternated doing light retreat with practice in the dark.

Her friend Padma Yangkyi took Rainbow Body (*see Chapter 11*) and Togden Semnyi died at the age of 85, leaving sacred relics in his ashes as a sign of his realization.

At the age of 14, together with his mother and sister, Chögyal Namkhai Norbu met Ayu Khandro, as she was considered to be an embodiment of Vajrayogini.[fn15] He visited her in her tiny stone hut which had no windows. Although Ayu Khandro could obviously see clearly in the dark, a single butter lamp was lit for the benefit of her guests. Although she was 113 years old, according to Chögyal Namkhai Norbu,

'She did not look particularly ancient. She had very long hair that reached her knees. It was black at the tips and white at the roots. Her hands looked like the hands of a young woman.'[16]

He spent two months with her receiving teachings, including the complete cycle of Dzogchen *Yangtig* teachings (*see Chapter 11*) and her own Mind *terma* of the lion-headed Dakini Simhamukha. She became one of his main teachers.

At the age of 115, without showing any signs of illness, Ayu Khandro left her body. After two weeks, her body shrank and became very small. Her death was in the middle of winter but despite this, suddenly there was a thaw and trees and flowers bloomed. She left behind lots of tiny relics, or *ringsel*.[16]

FOOTNOTES

[fn1] The three worlds of existence are the desire realm, the form realm and the formless.

[fn2] Guru Dragpo is a wrathful manifestation of Guru Rinpoche.

[fn3] *Vima Nyingthig, Bima Nyingthig* (*bi ma snying thig*), 'Innermost Teachings of Vimalamitra', one of four parts of the *nyingthig yazhi* (*snying thig ya bzhi*), compiled and partly written by Longchenpa.

[fn4] *Khandro Nyingthig* (*mkha' 'gro snying thig*), 'Innermost Teachings of the Dakinis', one of four parts of the *nyingthig yazhi* (*snying thig ya bzhi*), compiled and partly written by Longchenpa.

[fn5] Dorje Legpa (*rdo rje legs pa*): One of the principal Dzogchen protectors who is seated on a lion or sometimes a goat. He is known as 'the Good Vajra' and can be approached for help with mundane matters as well as with spiritual progress.

[fn6] *Dungsel* (*gdung ring bsrel*): Tiny pearl-like relics.

[fn7] *Longchen Nyingthig* (*klong chen snying thig*), 'Innermost Essence of the Great Expanse', terma teachings of Jigme Lingpa.

[fn8] Thangtong Gyalpo (*thang stong rgyal po*) (1385–1509) was an enlightened master famous for his building of nearly 60 suspension bridges. He also built temples strategically placed on specific geomantic points to repel armies invading Tibet.

[fn9] Drigung Kagyu (*'bri gung bka' brgyud*) is a sub-sect of the Phagdru Kagyud tradition, founded by Phagmodrupa Dorje Gyalpo in the twelfth century.

fn10 *Tsa lung (rtsa lung)* is a general term for yogic methods used to control energy channels and *prana*.

fn11 The first Karmapa founded the Karma Kagyudpa sect in the twelfth century. This has been a strong living tradition until today, guided by the presence of successive reincarnations of the Gyalwa Karmapas.

fn12 Tai Situ Rinpoche is recognized as an incarnation of Maitreya and his first incarnation was in the fourteenth century. There has always been a very close relationship between the Karmapas and the Tai Situ reincarnations.

fn13 Shabdrung Rinpoche or Ngawang Namgyal (*ngag dbang rnam rgyal*) (1594–1651) was the founder of the state of Bhutan.

fn14 *Prana* (Skt) (Tib. *lung*) disease refers to a disorder of the winds in the energy channels of the body.

fn15 Vajrayogini (Skt) Dorje Naljorma (Tib.) (*rdo rje rnal 'byor ma*): An important enlightened Dakini found in all the schools of Tibetan Buddhism. She is semi-wrathful in form and red, indicating her association with passion.

fn16 *Ringsel (ring bsrel)*: Tiny relic pills of sacred substance found in the ashes after the cremation of a practitioner who has reached a certain level of realization.

CHAPTER 9

VISIONS AND TERMA

'Treasure-finders of all sorts will appear continuously,
And treasure-doctrines will pour forth like spores
from mushrooms.
None of them will fail to bear fruit;
They will be reminders of me, Orgyen.'[1]

THE TERMA TRADITION

While the *kama* tradition is known as 'the long transmission', the *terma* tradition is the 'short transmission' lineage particular to the Tantric and Dzogchen paths.

Terma are hidden treasure teachings which were concealed by Padmasambhava and his consort Yeshe Tsogyal in the ninth century to be rediscovered by reincarnations of his original disciples when the conditions were favourable. For more than 100 years after Padmasambhava's departure Yeshe Tsogyal concealed vast numbers of *terma* in Tibet. Some were also hidden by Vairocana, Vimalamitra and others.

There are generally two kinds of treasures: Earth Treasures (*sa ter*) and Mind Treasures (*gong ter*). The kind of hidden treasure teachings known as Earth *terma* are found in lakes, mountains, temples, trees, rocks, even the sky, and take the form of yellow scrolls of paper on which is written the secret script of the dakinis. Earth *terma* can also be sacred objects. Guru Rinpoche said that except 'for a dog's corpse, anything can be taken out as *ter*'.[2] In other words, the precious teachings can manifest in an infinite number of ways. Earth *terma* are held in safekeeping by the dakinis or protectors of the teachings. As removing sacred objects from the land can harm the energy of the earth, Earth Treasures can be transformed into Mind Treasures when necessary.

Mind *terma* are teachings that Padmasambhava transmitted to the minds of his realized disciples. He predicted the time when each of his 25 principal disciples would take birth and which particular *terma* teachings they would discover. Sometimes the same *terma* would be hidden in the minds of several disciples, but generally each would be held in the mind of one person. Mind *terma* are reawakened by symbolic scripts, which act as a cipher to unlock them. As such they are not physical texts or objects, but mind teachings, concealed until revealed through symbols, visions or dreams. This means that they are not subject to the same physical risks as Earth *terma* and remain safe until they are discovered. The key to their revelation may be only a single seed syllable, perhaps just one or two Tibetan or Sanskrit words, or it can be script in the language of the dakinis, which can only be understood by highly realized beings or those who hold the transmission of that particular *terma*. Even fragments of text may act as a trigger to the visionary revelation of the complete text.

It was Yeshe Tsogyal, with her infallible memory and complete devotion, who was entrusted with Padmasambhava's teachings. He told her:

'[From] beginningless time, I have hidden many precious and sacred dharma teachings. These are inexhaustible and will continue in the future until samsara is completely emptied of beings ... You, my lady, must take pains to procure all my profound treasures.'[3]

She wrote down all his teachings, with some help, on five different kinds of yellow scrolls of paper (symbolizing the five Buddha families). In fact although the scrolls are always referred to in *terma* revelations as yellow scrolls, they are not always yellow but can be other colours. They were placed in caskets made from different substances such as wood, clay or exquisite jewels and entrusted to the care of the dakinis or *terma* protectors for concealment. Once sealed, they were completely closed and showed not even a hairline crack where they could be prised open.

Sometimes treasure teachings were hidden physically by Padmasambhava and Yeshe Tsogyal when they visited sacred places; at other times they were concealed from a distance or kept hidden by protectors of the teachings in different regions. If an area is physically under threat at any time, *terma* teachings may be moved elsewhere. Ever relevant, they can also be hidden today to bring benefit to countless future beings.

In some cases, teachings are discovered and then reconcealed to be revealed at a later date. Thus *terma* have a particular power and immediacy, as well as being directly relevant and appropriate to the time and place they are found. In this way, the *terma* tradition keeps teachings fresh for each new generation. According to Padmasambhava,

> *'In the defiled age the teaching's limit*
> *Will be preserved by treasures.'*[4]

Terma also help keep the purity of the transmission intact, since misunderstandings and errors arise more easily in a long transmission. Jigme Lingpa said that *terma* teachings appear when the teachings 'are adulterated like milk at a fair ... For the *terma* are unadulterated and are the swift path of practice.'[5] With *terma*, the teachings are always kept alive, the blessings stay potent and a direct line of transmission is maintained.

Some teachings are concealed and then placed under the protection of fierce and powerful non-human beings such as the maroon-coloured Ekajati[fn1], the Queen of the Mamos,[fn2] the chief protector of the Dzogchen teachings, or the dark reddish-brown thousand-eyed and terrifying Rahula, the Wild God of the Skies.[fn3] The teachings are then handed over by the protectors to the appointed person, or *terton*, at a later date. Some non-human protectors come from other classes of beings who were bound to protect the teachings by Padmasambhava. They can also be enlightened Buddhas manifesting in the form of non-humans.

It is important that a *terma* is kept secret at the time of discovery and often for some time afterwards, even a number of years. It is only revealed much sooner if the dakinis and protectors indicate to the *terton* that the time is right.

THE CONSORT

The support of a chosen consort is considered very important for the discovery of hidden teachings, which is why lamas who were destined to become *tertons* were generally householders and not monastics. The wisdom bliss generated by union with a consort acts as an aid to the revelation of *terma* and can increase the lifespan of the lama. Sometimes the dakinis manifest in human form to enable a male *terton* to find his treasure. Conversely, for a female *terton*, a male consort is necessary.

The consort is therefore not viewed in the ordinary sense as a source of sensual delight, but as a means of producing the union of bliss and emptiness, without attachment. Terdag Lingpa, for example, was able to receive the guidance for the *terma* of 'The Destroyer of Arrogance', *Yamantaka*, through his union with a dakini. She appeared to him in a dream in the form of a beautiful young lady colourfully bedecked in silk, wearing precious jewels, 'showing him the expression and indications of great bliss. By having union with her he was liberated into the expanse of freedom from elaborations, the nature of the experiences of exquisite great bliss.'⁶ She placed her ring in his cup. When he awoke, the ring had transformed into a light red scroll with a script: the guide to the *terma*.

Sometimes the consort can be an unlikely figure. They are not always young and beautiful! One Nyingma lama who was predicted to be a treasure-finder prayed for one week for his consort to appear. When she did, it was in the shape of a terrifying and ragged old woman, blind in one eye, cutting wood. Fortunately, he recognized her as an emanation of the fierce one-eyed Dzogchen protector Ekajati and knew her to be the dakini who had appeared in answer to his prayers! She duly became his consort and he lived to discover countless hidden treasure teachings. In another instance a crippled old woman, unable to walk, was the support for a young *terton* to reveal a hidden teaching. The consort of Mingyur Dorje, a famous *terton*, was dumb. As she could not communicate, the only way he could write his *terma* down was by wearing her ring. Without it, he could not write!

At other times, if a *terton* cannot meet his right consort, his life might be cut short or his *terma* not propagated. Karma

Lingpa (1327–1387) was one such treasure-finder who died young because he lacked the favourable connection with his prophesied consort.

More recently, Dilgo Khyentse Rinpoche (1910–1991), an incarnation of the great nineteenth-century *terton* Jamyang Khyentse Wangpo, while a young man in retreat at a place called White Grove, became 'seriously ill. Khyentse Chokyi Lodro and many other lamas were of the unanimous opinion that the time had come for him to take a consort, as was necessary for him as a *terton* ... So he married Lhamo, a simple girl from an ordinary farming family. From then on his health improved; he had many deep visions and revealed several mind treasures.'[7] He had not seemed at all interested in getting married, but his lamas had told him to do so otherwise he would die. His wife, Khandro Lhamo, was brought to him by the lamas. She recalls their meeting:

'Rinpoche was very ill and his face looked dark. I was worried to see him so sick and thought he was going to die. But after my arrival his health seemed to improve. One day he was up and about in his white robe, and he asked me to come and eat with him ... In some texts it was predicted that Rinpoche should marry me to ensure that his activities for the Buddhadharma would become very vast.'[8]

TERTONS

There are said to be 100 major *tertons* and hundreds of minor *tertons*. A major or great *terton* is defined by Terdag Lingpa as 'one who discovers a complete cycle of teachings through which someone may gain complete enlightenment'. They must have discovered *terma* not only relating to Dzogchen but also to Padmasambhava and the Buddha of Compassion, Avalokiteshvara. A great *terton* must be realized through the Great Perfection of Dzogchen and therefore cannot discover false teachings.

Of the 100 major *tertons*, there are five known as *terton* kings. These are Guru Chowang, the consort of Jomo Menmo; Pema Lingpa, who lived in the fifteenth century; Jamyang Khyentse Wangpo, who died just before the turn of the twentieth century; Dorje Lingpa (*see below*) and Nyang Nyima Odzer.

It is also worth noting that besides those marvellous and genuine *tertons* there are also false *tertons* who make claims to their power in order to increase their wealth or status. In general, though, there are safeguards against false claims, such as writing out the revelation of a Mind *terma* twice and seeing how closely the two versions correspond to each other.

EARLY TERTONS

Jomo Menmo

Jomo Menmo was a renowned female *terton* who lived in the thirteenth century and was recognized as an incarnation of Yeshe Tsogyal. At the age of 13, while out grazing the family cattle, she dozed off near a sacred cave where Padmasambhava had meditated a few hundred years before. A melodious song awoke her, revealing a secret entrance to the cave, which she entered, only to find the terrifying sight of dakinis in a cremation ground, surrounded by decaying corpses. In the centre of the dakinis was the sow-headed red wisdom dakini Vajra Varahi. Strangely, Jomo Menmo felt no fear at all. Vajra Varahi addressed her:

'You are of the dakini race, child, like all women. Are you unaware of your own pristine Buddha-nature? You are perfectly free, liberated since the beginningless beginning. Dare to actualize that inherent freedom, beyond doubt and hesitation. The entire universe is your body, all beings your mind.'⁹

Placing the text *Gathering of All the Secrets of the Dakinis* on her head, Jomo Menmo instantly understood its entire teaching, even though it was written in the language of the dakinis. Vajra Varahi prophesied that she would attain enlightenment through the secret practice of this text:

'By realizing its blessing she will be naturally liberated ... all her associates will be conveyed to the level of supreme bliss, and will obtain enlightenment, not leaving a trace of their bodies.'¹⁰

Thereafter spontaneous wisdom dawned in the young woman's mind and she began to act in a free and crazy manner, singing mystical songs and speaking telepathically. Although some people had faith in her, most people thought her mad and said she had been possessed by a demoness, hence her name, Jomo Menmo, 'She who is Possessed by a Menmo Spirit'. Disturbed by the gossip, Jomo Menmo went off travelling and met her consort, the famous *terton* Guru Chowang. Through union with her, he was able to bring forth a *terma* which had hitherto been indecipherable.

Later, through his contact with Jomo Menmo, a siddha known as Lingje Repa attained vast realization and became very famous throughout India and Tibet. Secretly, Jomo Menmo benefited many beings, travelling around Tibet for 22 years.

At the age of 36, she left this world in a miraculous fashion. In the company of two other yoginis, she performed a feast offering on a mountaintop in central Tibet and then, to the utter astonishment of local herders, the three flew off into the sky and disappeared. It is said that they went to the dakini paradise of Padmasambhava's Copper-Coloured Mountain.

Jomo Menmo's *terma*, *Gathering of All the Secrets of the Dakinis*, was not propagated in her lifetime, as the time was not auspicious, and was hidden by the dakinis for more than 150 years, to be rediscovered by the great *terton* Pema Lingpa. In his previous life, he had been Guru Chowang, Jomo Menmo's consort. Such is the magical weaving and interweaving of this hidden treasure tradition.

THE GREAT LINGPAS

Padma Lingpa

One of the great five *terton* kings was Padma Lingpa, who lived in the fifteenth century. Blessed by Guru Rinpoche at the age of 26 with a list of 108 treasure troves, he found his first treasure in Lake Mebar. Fearlessly entering the lake with a burning lamp, he emerged from the water with the lamp still alight, carrying a great chest of treasure.

This prolific *terton* not only discovered texts but also sacred objects, gems, mirrors, deity images, *stupas* and in one case even a whole temple. Sadly, though, he was not able to discover more than half of the named 108 treasures, and it was up to his son to reveal some of the minor treasure teachings.

Dorje Lingpa

Dorje Lingpa (1346–1405) was the third of the five great *terton* kings and had seven visions of Guru Rinpoche at the age of 12. He discovered 108 treasures, including 43 great treasure troves, and actually met both Guru Rinpoche and Yeshe Tsogyal. Yeshe Tsogyal gave him long-life water from Yanglesho in Nepal, a wish-fulfilling gem and teachings. When he died, his sanctity was such that his corpse did not decay for three years and continued to speak.

Ratna Lingpa

The other great Lingpas were Sangye Lingpa (1340–1396) and Ratna Lingpa. Ratna Lingpa (1403–1479) was a very important treasure-holder who also ensured the continuation of the *kama* tradition. He said to have discovered so many *terma* that he accomplished the work of three lifetimes in one! From the age of 10, he had pure visions and at 27 first met Guru Rinpoche (in a vision) wearing a yellow hat and robe. In all he had 25 visions of Guru Rinpoche and visited his pure realm, the Copper-Coloured Mountain.

Terdag Lingpa

A prolific seventeenth-century Nyingma *terton* was Terdag Lingpa, who was considered an emanation of Vairocana, the Great Translator. At the age of only 10, he had a vision of Padmasambhava and later he had visionary contact with count-less deities, including Vajrasattva and Vajrayogini. He was empowered in his discovery of treasure teachings not only by Padmasambhava directly but also by others, including Yeshe Tsogyal, Vimalamitra and Vairocana.

Sometimes *terma* are physically difficult to find and tools such as hammers and chisels are required to prise them out of rocks. But Terdag Lingpa received the *terma* of the deity Yamantaka[fn4] with considerable ease. Rainbow lights indicated its whereabouts in high inaccessible rock on a steep mountainous slope. Terdag Lingpa was so afraid of heights that he could not even bear to look at it! Becoming unconscious with fear, he found himself transported in an instant to a 'tent-like cave, with walls like crystal coloured with bright frescoes. In that cave were a young and beautiful lady and a handsome man, both dressed in exquisite white clothing ... The lady gave him two scrolls and the man a three-cornered casket ...'[11] Once again outside the cave he fainted with fear and when he came to, he found himself down below the precipitous rock, on a mountain pathway.

Terdag Lingpa was not only the disciple but also the teacher of the Great Fifth Dalai Lama. Also known as Minling Terchen, he founded the famous Nyingma monastery of Mindroling where, with his brother Dharmashri, he gathered together and published all the Nyingma *kama* and his own *terma*.

It was not until the nineteenth century that a thorough compilation of *terma*, including most of the essential root *terma*, was assembled by Jamyang Khyentse Wangpo and Jamgon Kongtrul: the *Rinchen Terdzod*, a massive work which today comprises over 63 volumes.

Chogyur Lingpa

Chogyur Lingpa (1829–1871) was a great treasure-finder of Tibet who came into this world heralded by rainbow light and other auspicious omens. Guru Rinpoche appeared to him in his early teens and prophesied that he would be 'especially sublime in the world'.[12]

One day, sitting in a temple drinking tea, Chogyur Lingpa had a vision of Yeshe Tsogyal. To everyone's amazement, without warning, he jumped off his throne and leapt onto his horse. Galloping off with his attendants in hot pursuit, he rode straight into a torrential river, where he completely disappeared, to the dismay of everyone. Fortunately, after only a matter of minutes he emerged on the other riverbank, carrying a yellow scroll. While he had been drinking tea, Yeshe Tsogyal had told him that she had entrusted a treasure teaching hundreds of years earlier to a gigantic crocodile! That very day, a full moon, the crocodile's mouth guarding the treasure would close at midday, not to reopen for another 60 years! It was imperative that these teachings were retrieved instantly, as they were very much needed at that time. So, just before midday, Chogyur Lingpa retrieved the sacred scroll from the teeth of the crocodile! The crocodile was a protector of the teachings who had been bound by Padmasambhava centuries earlier to safeguard the *terma*:

'*According to the Lotus-Born Guru's prophecy ... the* terma *contained teachings on wrathful deity practices suitable for the turbulent times in which Chogyur Lingpa lived; he was the one teacher who could practise and propagate those teachings.*'[13]

Once the mystical dakini script was deciphered, Chogyur Lingpa practised these teachings and then spread them throughout Tibet, bringing freedom to many people.

Jamyang Khyentse Wangpo (1820–1892)

Jamyang Khyentse Wangpo held all the lineages of Tibetan Buddhism as well as Bon and was known as the fifth *terton* king. In childhood, he could remember his previous lives and showed

extraordinary intelligence, understanding books after only seeing them once.

At the age of eight, he became seriously ill, but his obstacles
were removed by a vision of Guru Rinpoche and Yeshe Tsogyal.
When he was 15, in a visionary state, he travelled to Bodhgaya in
India, where he met Manjusrimitra, surrounded by great stacks
of books. Manjusrimitra blessed him with two key teachings,
the *Prajnaparamita*[fn5] and a Dzogchen text which dissolved into
his heart. Still in this visionary state, he found himself facing a
fire, which he had no choice but to enter. At that moment his
body was burnt and purified into a shining body of light, and he
realized that he was the same being as Vimalamitra.

At 24, he remembered that he had been the great lama
Chetsun Senge Wangchuk, who had passed away in a Body of
Light (*see Chapter 11*). This realization awakened his knowledge
of the *Chetsun Nyingthig* teachings.[fn6]

When he was 40 years old, Guru Rinpoche, in the form of the
great *terton* Sangye Lingpa, gave him a text. At that moment
Jamyang Khyentse understood all the revealed treasures that had
been revealed or would appear in Tibet, and was able to see all the
treasure-holders. He thus became their authorized successor.

Jamyang Khyentse had numerous visions, including that of
White Tara, and received teachings of all the Tibetan lineages
from over 150 masters and scholars. His activity was vast,
publishing sacred texts and writing several hundred works, as
well as building temples and libraries, and sponsoring the building of *stupas* and statues. His sanctity was such that at the
Jokhang temple in Lhasa, 100 butter lamps lit themselves spontaneously and rice he offered turned into white flowers. The
third Dodrupchen said of him:

'Wherever he lived, a very strong sweet scent always filled the surroundings ... you would always feel a pleasant heat, as if from a fire in the cold. ... He was exceptionally caring of poor people and spoke to them very gently ... He taught all kinds of assemblies with great confidence, like a lion.'[14]

At the age of 73 he passed away, leaving behind disciples in all the lineages, including the fourteenth and fifteenth Karmapas. For us today, Jamyang Khyentse's most enduring gift is his complete openness to and mastery of all the precious teachings in Tibet, regardless of school and lineage, and his non-sectarian approach.

CONTEMPORARY TERTONS

Dudjom Rinpoche

Dudjom Rinpoche was a formidable *terton* who passed away as recently as 1987. His previous incarnation, Trakthung Dudjom Lingpa, was a powerful crazy siddha and a great *terton*, a practitioner of Vajra Kilaya. Although a finder of vast numbers of hidden treasure teachings, he was almost illiterate and required the aid of 13 scribes to write down his *terma*, which were known as 'New Treasures'. He predicted that the New Treasures would spread all round the world, particularly to the West.

Dudjom Rinpoche, his reincarnation, was an enlightened lama, a great *terton* and scholar who wrote extensive commentaries on his predecessor's revealed treasure teachings as well as his own. His first major work on the precious Dzogchen teachings was written when he was only 17 years old.

Chögyal Namkhai Norbu

One of the great *tertons* teaching tirelessly on this earth today is Chögyal Namkhai Norbu. Those who are fortunate enough to have contact with him know of his extreme clarity regarding his dreams. One *terma* that he has widely disseminated is connected with long life and the dakini Mandarava, who was one of Guru Rinpoche's main consorts. *The Practice of Long Life of the Immortal Dakini Mandarava* is simultaneously both a Mind Treasure and connected to pure vision. This *terma* was revealed to Chögyal Namkhai Norbu over a short period in 1984, starting with a pure vision at Tharling monastery in the Himalayas, and was completed through a series of dreams at the cave of Maratika in Nepal where Mandarava and Guru Rinpoche had achieved immortality with the long-life practice of Amitayus.

It was Chögyal Namkhai Norbu's uncle, Jamyang Chokyi Wangchuk[fn7], who appeared to him in a dream, saying that once he reached Maratika with his students, he should practise the long-life practice of immortality, and he gave him the seed syllables of the five dakinis. Four days later, another dream revealed the seed syllables of the dakinis, *BAM HA RI NI SA*, in concentric circles of radiant light – white, blue, yellow, red and green, the colours of the five elements. From the central letter, *BAM*, an explosion revealed these verses:

'*The Long Life Practice of the Immortal Dakini*
The Sphere of the Vital Essence of the Vajra
It has been sealed.'[15]

A few days later, while Chögyal Namkhai Norbu was sleeping with his head outside the tent, these same verses appeared in the sky. From the central sphere of light, the root text started appearing in the form of shining golden letters and Chögyal Namkhai Norbu read it through three times. When he woke up, the text was clear in the sky in the form of luminous letters.

In another dream, Ekajati, the Dakini Queen, protector of Dzogchen and *terma*, indicated that the writing of this Mind Treasure would be of great benefit to Chögyal Namkhai Norbu's disciples. Chögyal Namkhai Norbu wrote the text down twice during a period of three days and it was checked by his sister, the Dzogchen yogini Jamyang Chodron, and some of his students who understood Tibetan. This is a way of checking that a *terma* is authentic. The only difference between the texts was one phrase referring to the immortal *vajra* body. Ekajati gave permission to disseminate this teaching and it was transmitted immediately at the cave of Maratika and is now practised worldwide by thousands of practitioners. Such is the wonder of *terma* and the process of their revelation.

PROPHETIC DREAMS

The discovery of a *terma* may be heralded some time beforehand through a significant dream. In the case of Chögyal Namkhai Norbu, a *terma* related to the Dance of the Vajra was first signified in a dream he had in Singapore six or seven years before the *terma* was revealed.

In the dream, Chögyal Namkhai Norbu was in China with many young people. They were walking up a mountain towards a white rock that was shining as if the place was important. He wondered what this indicated and asked the Chinese girl walking alongside him. She said that this was a monastery of a lama called Kangkar Rinpoche. Kangkar Rinpoche was one of Chögyal Namkhai Norbu's teachers who had had many students in China. In the dream they went up to the monastery. An old Chinese lady at the door gave Chögyal Namkhai Norbu a piece of paper with Chinese writing on it which he could not read easily. He thought she was asking him for money to go inside, but this was not the case. They went into the monastery:

'... *and there was a large statue made out of white stone like alabaster. I looked and thought it was a Green Tara but it was not. But it had writing on it in both Chinese and Tibetan on the plinth – it was a statue of Gomadevi [a princess who was an important Dzogchen teacher]. I thought it was very strange that a monastery of Kangkar Rinpoche had a statue of Gomadevi in it because there was no obvious connection.*'[16]

There was nothing else in the hall at all, just this large statue. On the right there was a staircase and Chögyal Namkhai Norbu climbed up to the level of the statue's knees.

'*I leant forward to touch my forehead to the statue and make an invocation, and I saw that in the left hand on her lap there was a large crystal ball. I looked at it and I saw within it a light shining and moving around – like the statue was alive. I was very surprised by this.*'[17]

Later others asked him who the statue was and he replied it was Gomadevi.

'*Then we sat and sang "The Song of the Vajra" ... After this dream, I had other dreams of Gomadevi, in Italy and in America. Gomadevi is connected with the Dance of the Vajra; she was a princess in Oddiyana and is in the transmission lineage of Dzogchen* Semde. *She is also very important in* Anuyoga. *These dreams took place directly before the* terma *of the dance was received.*'[18]

The Dance of the Vajra is a *terma* of Chögyal Namkhai Norbu, a treasure teaching that was revealed to him through a series of dreams over a number of years, starting in the 1980s. The teaching was transmitted to him by Gomadevi, daughter of the king of Oddiyana, who had received teachings from Garab Dorje. The Dance of the Vajra, like 'The Song of the Vajra', is related to the state of contemplation and is therefore a primary practice in Dzogchen. Wherever it is danced, it has a harmonizing effect on the surrounding area or land. Most profoundly, it is a path in itself, leading to real knowledge of the self-perfected state and to total realization.

FOOTNOTES

[fn1] Ekajati is the main guardian of the Dzogchen teachings. Her name means 'One Single Birth'. She is usually depicted as maroon in colour, with one eye, one tooth, one breast and one tuft of hair, to symbolize non-duality. Although she manifests as a Mamo and rules over this class, she is not actually a Mamo herself but a realized guardian.

[fn2] Mamos (*ma mo*): One of the Eight Classes of spirits who can cause negativity and obstacles. Mamos generally control epidemics like cholera and can create war if they are seriously disturbed or offended.

[fn3] Rahula is one of the principal guardians of the Dzogchen teachings. His upper body is covered with eyes which enable him to see in all directions. He can manifest as balls of light in the sky, meteors or even UFOs.

[fn4] Yamantaka (*gshin rje gshed dregs 'joms*) is the wrathful manifestation of Manjushri, the Bodhisattva of Wisdom.

[fn5] The *Prajna Paramita* are a cycle of Sutras, part of the Mahayana teachings revealed by Nagarjuna, the Indian master who founded the Madhyamika philosophy otherwise known as 'the Middle Way'.

[fn6] *Chetsun Nyingthig* (*lce btsun snying thig*), 'Innermost Essence of Chetsun', a *terma* teaching.

[fn7] Jamyang Chokyi Wangchug (*'Jam dbyangs Chos kyi dBang phyug*) (1910–1963), teacher and uncle of Chögyal Namkhai Norbu.

CHAPTER 10

DREAMS AND DEATH

'The symbol-producing function of our dreams is an attempt to bring our original mind back to consciousness, where it has never been before, and where it has never undergone critical self-reflection.'[1]

Dreams have been used as a means of inner spiritual guidance for thousands of years in both the East and the West. At one time, all early cultures paid respect to this intrinsic aspect of human existence and developed their own traditions. The importance of dreams as a guide to the inner life was particularly prominent in ancient Egypt and Greece, and it still is in the American Indian, Aboriginal and Senoi cultures. Early Egyptian priests, who were known as 'masters of the secret things', systematically interpreted dreams as messages from the gods, while in ancient Greece, the initiates of the oracle Aesclepius induced healing dreams within a ritual context. The use of dreams as a specific means of monitoring or assessing an individual's spiritual development or condition is also well documented in the Tibetan Buddhist tradition.

In the West, an interest in dreams has come to the fore within the last century through the popularity of psychotherapy, particularly through the work of Sigmund Freud and Carl Gustav Jung. Freud called dreams 'the royal road to the unconscious', while Jung took their significance much further, owing to the fact that he included a religious dimension to the psyche.

DREAM INTERPRETATION

Dream interpretation can take different forms and be used for a range of purposes. In the life story of Milarepa, for example, Marpa asks all his disciples to watch their dreams one particular night in order to discern who is to continue the lineage:

'In this lineage I have the power to direct your practice by indications from dreams and omens. Therefore go and await your dreams. Remain watchful and aware of them.' [2]

That night all Marpa's foremost disciples have outstanding dreams, but none of them relates to the future of the lineage. Milarepa, however, has a dream of a huge mountain like Mount Meru. It is at the centre of the world and is encircled by four great pillars:

> *'Upon the eastern pillar crouched a great snow lion with a flowing mane of turquoise;*
> *From the southern pillar a tigress roared, spreading her claws through the dense forests;*
> *Above the western pillar a giant eagle soared, gazing upward toward heaven;*
> *While in the north a vulture spread its wings above a nest of fledglings, and the sky became full of little birds.'* [3]

When Milarepa has finished relating the dream in full, Marpa is overjoyed and tells his wife to prepare a ritual feast to which all the disciples are invited. When they are all gathered together Marpa sings a song interpreting the dream, which reveals the future of the lineage. He sings of how the four animals signify his four main disciples, and of Milarepa, he sings:

> 'Mila is like the vulture
> whose outspread wings signify
> his realization of the secret instruction.
> Its eyrie in the steep cliff means
> that his life will be as hard as a rock.
> The vulture's fledgling shows that
> he will have a peerless spiritual son,
> And the small birds scattered in space
> represent his many disciples
> and the spread of his teachings far and wide.
> His gaze and flight towards heaven shows
> he will leave the world of birth and death
> and arrive in the realm of perfect freedom.
> If the words of this old man are prophetic
> it is a most favourable dream for us all.'[4]

The interpretation of such dreams however, requires considerable skill and experience. The Tibetan Bon lama Tenzin Wangyal Rinpoche describes how his teacher Lopon Tenzin Namdak used dreams as a way of assessing whether his students were ready for specific spiritual teachings:

'Some of the students remembered no dream, which was considered a sign of obstacles. Lopon had them begin appropriate purification practices and delayed the beginning of the teaching until

each student did have a dream ... I dreamt about a bus circumam-
bulating my teacher's house, although there is actually no road
there. In the dream, the bus conductor was my friend and I stood
beside him handing out tickets to each person that boarded the
bus. The tickets were pieces of paper that had the Tibetan syllable
'A' written on them ... at the time I did not know that 'A' was a
symbol of major significance in the Dzogchen teachings.' [5]

Dreams can be prophetic by nature and can give indications for
a particular action to be carried out as well as contain premoni-
tions of future events. For example, early one morning, while
Chögyal Namkhai Norbu was walking through the ruins of
Shang Shung Gonpa in Tibet, he recollected a dream from the
previous night. In his dream he had entered a temple and found
himself drawn to a corner of the building where there was a
small opening at floor level. He had felt compelled to reach
down into it, but had found nothing. Then he thrust the full
length of his arm into the hole and to his surprise extended his
arm further than its normal length! His fingers grasped hold of
something. When he withdrew his hand, he found he was holding a bright sacred object.

After he had woken up, he recognized the ruins of Shang
Shung Gonpa as the same temple he had seen in his dream.
Looking around, he was drawn to a cavity in the ruins, now
partly full of sand. Just as in the dream, he pushed his hand into
the opening. Reaching down the full length of his arm, he found
a small statuette buried deep beneath the rubble. It was a
Garuda, a powerful eagle grasping a snake in its talons and beak.
Its fire-like wings curved up around its head. According to tradition, a Garuda has the power to protect and cure serious illness.
Its origins go back to the earliest civilizations of Asia and especially to the area around Mount Kailash. Its very name was that

of the valley Chögyal Namkhai Norbu was about to enter – the Valley of the Garuda, or *Khyung-lung!*

DREAMS OF CLARITY

In Tibetan Buddhism dreams themselves are generally classified as being of two types: 'karmic dreams' or 'dreams of clarity'.

Karmic dreams, which most often occur during the first part of the night, are related to 'karmic traces' which we carry with us from our daily life (or even from past lives) and are dictated by our physical, emotional and mental disposition and propensity.

Dreams of clarity can manifest in a variety of different ways. Dreams which predict the future, reveal healing songs or remedies, or give advice about one's spiritual condition are all considered to fall into this category. *Terma* teachings which are revealed through dreams are very special dreams of clarity, having relevance to the lineage as a whole (*see Chapter 9*).

Dreams of clarity usually occur in the early hours of the morning when our sleep is lighter and less conditioned by everyday concerns. They often have a symbolic or 'archetypal' quality, and can inform the dreamer in a very precise way. Most people have experienced a dream which has something of this quality at some time in their life, a dream which perhaps contains a warning or some personal advice. An understanding or intuitive grasp of this type of individual dream can often be spontaneous and direct.

Some Tibetan masters, because of the stability of their meditative practice, are able to use dreams of clarity specifically for divination purposes. Dreams can thus provide a very real source of spiritual inspiration and guidance on a variety of different levels both within Tibetan Buddhism and other traditions.

Apart from instructing the individual dreamer, there is also a class of dreams which bring benefit to the people at large. Such dreams are common amongst tribal societies, and are usually revealed through a shaman or holy man or woman. The visionary leader of the Sioux Indians, Black Elk, for example, dreamt of a herb which could bring relief to his tribe:

'The night was old by now and soon I fell asleep. And as I slept I saw my people sitting sad and troubled all around a sacred tepee, and there were many who were sick. And as I looked on them and wept, a strange light leapt upward from the ground close by – a light of many colours, sparkling, with rays that touched the heavens. Then it was gone, and in the place from whence it sprang a herb was growing and I saw the leaves it had. And as I was looking at the herb so that I might not forget it, there was a voice that woke me, and it said: "Make haste. Your people need you."' [6]

For the Aborigines, the 'Dreamtime' is a place of creative inspiration and spiritual guidance. According to their myths, creative products such as songs or designs have come through dreams since time immemorial and continue to enrich their culture today. These artistic gifts are seen as originating from their ancestors, who are known as 'the Dreamings', as opposed to coming from a personal or individual source.

Dreams which reveal a dance, skill or song which is of value to the entire tribe are also common among the Senoi people of the Malay peninsula. Dreaming and dream interpretation form the very basis of their society and are the major focus of their intellectual and spiritual interest. But unlike most Western approaches to dreaming, their attitude to the dream world is pro-active! Children are taught how to respond and behave in their dreams correctly, so as to be able to resolve their inner conflicts and simultaneously bring benefit to their society as a whole:

'The Senoi believes that any human being, with the aid of his fellows, can outface, master and actually utilize all being and forces in the dream universe. His experiences lead him to believe that, if you co-operate with your fellows or oppose them with good will in the daytime, their images will eventually help you in their dreams, and that every person should and can become the supreme ruler and master of his own dream or spiritual universe, and can demand and receive the help, co-operation of all the forces there.' [7]

LUCID DREAMS

Don Juan, the Mexican shaman, used the technique of remembering to look at his hands as a way of bringing awareness into his dreams and thereby opening up the whole dreamscape to another dimension.

In the West, the process of being aware within a dream is known as 'lucid dreaming'. Lucid dreams are often characterized by a sense of clarity and a heightened appreciation of detail, colour and emotional tone. This area has been subjected to considerable scientific research over the last century which has confirmed that not only is the maintenance of awareness in dreams possible, but that it is also an experience which can be accessed by most people. Within the scientific domain, however, the art of lucid dreaming remains largely a theoretical study, whereas within Tibetan Buddhism it is utilized specifically as a means of developing one's spiritual practice.

In the Dzogchen tradition especially, rather than placing emphasis on the interpretation of dreams, a practitioner is encouraged to bring awareness into their dreams and then to work creatively with this knowledge. Eventually, the dreamer is able to maintain awareness from the moment of falling asleep, including the period prior to dreams arising, which is known as the 'natural light' phase, right up to the moment of awakening.

DZOGCHEN AND NIGHT PRACTICE

The practice of the night is considered extremely important in the Dzogchen tradition since so much of our life is spent sleeping. The night-time dimension presents a much more fluid reality than our normal waking life, if we are able to utilize it consciously, and is therefore a great aid to practice.

'In the waking state, one can only go out of a room by way of the door, but in the dream state, one can seemingly pass through solid walls. This experience of the dream state is very favourable for the overcoming of attachments in daily life, because one experiences directly the insubstantiality and unreality of everything.'[8]

Ultimately, our daytime reality is nothing more than a 'big dream', an insubstantial manifestation of our own energy like a reflection in a mirror, yet it appears solid and fixed. Actively discovering the illusory nature of the dream state brings this realization home in a very real way. Practitioners are therefore encouraged to gradually bring awareness into their dreams, then learn to work with different experiences within the dream state, such as flying, travelling to different places or even other dimensions!

However, although dreams of clarity are of great value and can help inform the dreamer in a variety of ways, to cling to the meaning of dreams or to attach too much importance to their significance can, in the longer term, become an obstacle on the Dzogchen path. What is thought to be more important is the ability to maintain awareness throughout the night, not only whilst dreaming but more specifically during the 'natural light' period. This is a principal practice in the Dzogchen teachings.

'When one falls asleep, one becomes disengaged from the karmic traces of the material body, the karmic traces of vision, and the karmic traces of mental functioning. These karmic traces, during the waking state, manifest as one's material body, the external appearances one perceives, and the functioning of one's mind respectively. Why do we speak of being dis-engaged? ... From one's falling asleep right up to the moment when one begins to dream, there is no functioning of the mind and one finds oneself in the real condition of existence. In this one will experience to a certain degree a merging with what is called the natural clear light.' [9]

When an individual is able to bring awareness into the state of the natural clear light, all discursive thoughts or dualistic notions which create distractions are absent. In dream practice, one is still working with images and visions actively, whereas in the clear light practice there is neither subject nor object, only non-dual *rigpa*. This is why dream yoga is considered to be a secondary practice in Dzogchen.

Many people say, however, they do not dream, or cannot remember their dreams, let alone bring awareness into dreams or the pre-dreaming state! If a person has a problem in this area, it is important to understand the causes underlying their condition. They may be sleeping too deeply or may be disturbed by an imbalance in their energy. They may be eating or drinking too much or too late at night, the room they are sleeping in may be too dark or too stuffy, or their breathing may be constrained. Gradually, by understanding the causes of the problem and then overcoming them, it is possible not only to remember many dreams but to also become lucid. There are also specific practices which can help the individual to develop this capacity. Although this can be difficult to achieve initially, it is an extremely important training not only for developing one's daily practice but also as a preparation for the moment of one's death.

DEATH AND THE BARDO

The process of falling asleep is compared to dying in Buddhism and therefore the night practice is considered an important preparation for death. In the Buddhist teachings, great importance is placed on the moment of death and what is known as the *bardo* state. Literally, the Tibetan term *bardo* means 'suspended between'. The *bardo* generally refers to the state of limbo between one lifetime and the next but can also refer to the period between our birth and death, known as the 'first *bardo*'. In the West, it is generally thought that since the body and consciousness are intimately related, when the body dies, consciousness also ceases to exist. This stands in sharp contrast to the ancient Buddhist notion of a continuity of consciousness based on the interrelatedness of death and rebirth.

The famous misnamed *Tibetan Book of the Dead* is part of a series of ancient teachings on the *bardo* from the time of Padmasambhava, which were subsequently revealed as a *terma* by Karma Lingpa in the fourteenth century. The original text *Bar do thos grol* literally means 'Self-Liberation through Hearing, during the Intermediate Period that Follows Death'. According to this text, our consciousness simply sheds its outworn frame at death, much like a snake sheds its skin, and then continues through the intermediary *bardo* state until it takes on a new body, i.e. is reincarnated.

There are many recorded accounts of individuals who have entered the initial stages of dying, often described as entering a tunnel, and have returned to life again with a clear recollection of what they witnessed. If an individual is able to maintain awareness throughout the whole process, in much the same way as during sleep, then it is possible to have control over one's future rebirth rather than being simply driven by the 'winds of *karma*' into another life. In other words, the moment of death is an important moment in which the individual can achieve total liberation from the round of suffering in *samsara* rather than simply being propelled unconsciously through confusion, fear or other emotional tendencies.

There are broadly speaking four *bardo* states (although the *Union of Sun and Moon Tantra* adds an additional two, that of dreams and that of the state of *samadhi*, which are incorporated into the 'first *bardo*'):

❋ The first is the natural *bardo* of this life, beginning at birth and ending at death (*rang bzhin bar do*).

❋ The second, the *bardo* of death (*'chi kha'i bar do*), is when the sense faculties dissolve or vanish.

❋ The third is that luminous period after death when sounds, lights and rays manifest, sometimes known as the period of 'quintessential reality' (*chos nyid bar do*).

❋ The fourth is the *bardo* of becoming, or the 'intermediate period of existence' (*srid pa bar do*) when *karma* manifests to draw a person back to rebirth in different samsaric states of being. This last phase is analogous to the onset of dreaming during the sleep state.

When we are alive, we have a material body which attracts all kinds of difficulties and obstacles. Once we are dead and no longer have our material body, our senses and consciousness are unobstructed and we therefore have more clarity and capacity to manifest our real potentiality. In Dzogchen, when we speak of the potentiality of an individual, we do so in terms of the functioning of sound, light and rays, not only in life as a reflection of one's mind, but also in the state of the *bardo*. At this point, if we have received transmission and done a practice such as Xitro, the practice of the peaceful and wrathful deities,[fn1] we can recognize the arising of these manifestations as a reflection of the clarity of our own enlightened state. Otherwise the sounds, lights and rays that arise will only serve as a cause for distraction or fear. Through Tantric practices such as extensive visualization of oneself in the form of a deity and mantric recitation, at the moment of death the deity can manifest and be a source of liberation.

'When one dies with presence, then in the chos nyid bar do, *all the apparitions which appear will simply arise as the manifestation of spontaneous self-perfection and one will recognize them as such. These spontaneously self-perfected qualities which appear are those of the Sambhogakaya. Falling asleep is an analogous process to dying, and so attaining mastery over the dream state in this life will allow one to realize mastery over death and the* bardo *state. Falling asleep in a state of the natural clear light is equivalent to the experience of the* chos nyid bar do.'[10]

During the *chos nyid bar do*, various Tantras speak of the arising of four or sometimes five lights: white, red, black and 'beyond thought'. This is the point when consciousness is just beginning to reawaken:

'There is the presence of the state of awareness, and yet mind has not begun to enter into operations such as thinking. This is the passage through which one moves in that state which is called the natural light ... In Tantrism, this period is also described as the moment in which one meets the mother light ... In the Dzogchen teaching, the last of these phases, the fifth light, is spoken of as lhundrup, *the state of self-perfectedness. In that moment you have a re-awakening of consciousness. It is possible for you to recognize that which has been transmitted to you through direct introduction by the teacher ... This knowledge is spoken of as the "son" knowledge, in comparison with the "mother" knowledge or full experience ... The analogy used is that of a son uniting with this mother.'* [11]

But even for those who do not practise in this lifetime, there is the chance of liberation through contact with a *tagdrol*. *Tag* means 'to wear something like an amulet or protection'; *drol* means 'self-liberation'. A *tagdrol* can be either a very important mantra like 'The Song of the Vajra', sacred letters or a printed mandala of mantras which are placed on the heart of a dying or dead person. If these are worn within the lifetime of a person, this also has great benefit, as it can aid liberation. For non-practitioners, it can create the possibility of meeting the teachings in the future.

FOOTNOTES

[fn1] Xitro (*shi khro*): Practice of peaceful and wrathful deities from *The Tibetan Book of the Dead*.

CHAPTER 11

REALIZATION AND THE RAINBOW BODY

'My heart leaps up when I behold
A rainbow in the sky:
So was it when my life began;
So be it now I am a man;
So be it when I shall grow old,
Or let me die! ...'[1]

In Dzogchen, supreme realization manifests through the Rainbow Body (*'ja' 'lüs*) or the Body of Light. The physical body seems to disappear, but actually dissolves into rainbow-coloured light, which is the essence of the five elements. This type of realization and the methods to achieve it are very precisely documented.

The notion of a body composed of light is not peculiar to Dzogchen, for it is also found throughout other spiritual traditions. For example, the death of Christ and his resurrection can be seen through his manifestation after death in the form of light. After his crucifixion, the linen clothes in which his body had been embalmed with aloes and myrrh were seen lying empty in the sepulchre in the garden by not only Mary Magdalene but also Simon Peter and another disciple. The body of Jesus had completely vanished. The cloth napkin that had been around his head was now somewhere else. 'For as yet they knew not the scripture, that he must rise again from the dead.'[2] Jesus first appeared to Mary Magdalene – 'he, a little pale still from the grave, disburdened came to her: in all parts resurrected'[3] – and later that evening to a gathering of his disciples, showing his hands and sides with their marks. To the doubting Thomas, one of his 12 apostles, he manifested again as proof of his existence, and then later at the Sea of Tiberias. 'And many other signs truly did Jesus in the presence of his disciples, which are not written in this book.'[4]

The Sufi master Pir Vilayat Khan, speaking of Hildegard of Bingen, recounts her saying that what we need to do is 'to discover that we are essentially a being of light'.[5] This eleventh-century visionary, who established her own exclusively female convent, was a completely down-to-earth woman and at the same time 'totally immersed in this world of light'.[6] Pir Vilayat argues that there is no such thing as death because at the physical level of the body, electrons 'never die. They live forever even if one is incinerated and this is true of the protons. Electrons also get transmuted into photons, so ultimately one becomes a being of light.'[7]

RAINBOW BODY AND THE GREAT TRANSFER

In Tibet, particularly in the Dzogchen lineage, there are a number of accounts of spiritual practitioners attaining realization and manifesting Rainbow Body or the Body of Light and, through their supreme compassion, manifesting at will in the form of a light body to different classes of beings. Remarkable tales of such manifestations are not just expressions of fantasy and myth, for this type of realization is based on very specific practices and forms of training found within the Dzogchen tradition.

'A practitioner who manifests this realization cannot really be said to have "died" at all, in the ordinary sense of the word because he or she still remains spontaneously active as a principle of being in a Body of Light. The spontaneous activity of such an individual will be directed for the benefit of others, and he or she is actually visible to someone in a physical body who has sufficient clarity.'[8]

The first four masters of the Dzogchen lineage in our world, the *Rigdzin* or *Vidyadharas* Garab Dorje, Manjushrimitra, Sri Singha and Jnanasutra, all took Rainbow Body at the time of their death, but in response to their students' anguished pleas, they reappeared in a blaze of rainbow light, leaving their last testaments.

Dzogchen masters who have the capacity to realize Rainbow Body have understood the functioning of energy. If the state of the individual is seen as a crystal, then there is no external reality such as rays and lights reflecting from the crystal: they simply emanate from the crystal, which is the state of *rigpa*. With this capacity, masters are then able to integrate all pure and impure visions into the state of *rigpa*. There is no longer any separation between external and internal. The individual has completely overcome the notion of duality, subject and object. As such they are able to manifest Rainbow Body.

'[When] one fully discovers and manifests one's own nature, one is discovering and manifesting the nature of the universe. The existence of duality is nothing but an illusion, and when this illusion is undone the primordial inseparability of the individual and the universe is fully discovered ... the Body of Light manifests.'[9]

The methods used in Dzogchen to attain Rainbow Body are found in the *Longde* and *Upadesha* series, through visions which arise in contemplation. Once one has entered the third level of these visions, one's body enters the dimension of light at death. This usually takes about seven days but may sometimes take longer, and if interrupted, the body shrinks to a very small size. Once the body has completely dissolved into the essence of its elements, all that is left behind is hair and fingernails, which are considered impurities, gross elements of the physical body. Any individual who achieves this state has moved beyond the state of death and can manifest for the sake of others through the Rainbow Body.

A practitioner who completes the fourth level of visions does not have to wait for physical death to enter into the essence of the elements, but can accomplish this without any of the signs of a normal death. This is called 'the Great Transfer'. It is said that both Padmasambhava and Vimalamitra manifested this level of realization, as did Tapihritsa, the Bonpo master. Vimalamitra is said to have gone to the sacred Five-Peaked Mountain, *Wu-ta'i Shan*, in China and, according to Tulku Thondup:

'If your spiritual eyes are clear, you can see him in person at the Five Peaks. There are many incidents of seeing and receiving teachings from Vimalamitra at the Five Peaks. I heard many stories from my teacher Kyala Khenpo Rinpoche when I was young [but unless] you are an accomplished person, the best you can see of Vimalamitra is as a bird, a rainbow light, or an ordinary person and the like.' [10]

Like Vimalamitra, Padmasambhava also appears to practitioners who show him great devotion, not only in places which are sacred to him (like Tso Pema, Riwallsar, in northern India) but also in what may seem to be unlikely places such as Paris! Sadly, sometimes he is not always recognized. Dudjom Rinpoche told the story of the time when he had prayed ardently to Padmasambhava for a meaningful blessing to help him compose a prayer. The following morning, in a dream, he was sitting inside a large building like a temple when a musician 'dressed in white clothing and with long, flowing locks'[11] appeared. Playing the cymbals and dancing in clockwise spiralling steps, the musician came through the door and danced closer and closer to Dudjom Rinpoche, singing, 'If you wish to establish the Dharma, plant it in the heart. In the depths of the heart Buddhahood is found ...'[12] The sound of the cymbals increased in volume with each line of his song until they sounded so loudly at the end that Dudjom Rinpoche woke up. He remembered all the words and, with deep regret, realized that the musician was Guru Rinpoche himself and that he had not recognized him. With great devotion he then composed a prayer to his guru.

LONGDE AND YANGTIG

Longde and *Yangtig*[fn1] are two of the principal methods that lead to the realization of Rainbow Body.

Longde, the Series of Space, is a Dzogchen teaching which works through direct experience. It works with space and visions induced through the breath and particular meditative postures.

Vairocana first taught *Longde* in Tibet to an old man of 85, Pang Mipham Gonpo, who had diligently practised Tantric visualizations and mantra all his life but now wanted something to guarantee total realization. He was a simple man, not at all intellectual, and thought he had little time left. So Vairocana transmitted to him some essential *Longde* teachings. 'Becoming very joyful, the old man embraced his master about the neck and would not let go for a whole day!'[13] Despite being a bit decrepit, he was able to practise the teachings as Vairocana, to keep him stable, gave him a belt and stick, the use of which has passed down over generations. Pang Mipham went on to live for another 100 years in excellent health and subsequently attained Rainbow Body. Although he did not have many disciples himself and was not well known in his lifetime, for the next seven generations, his lineage of disciples attained Rainbow Body through *Longde* practice.

Yangtig are essential teachings of Dzogchen which involve doing practice in the dark in order to develop vision. Ayu Khandro (*see page 112*) spent more than 50 years in retreat in the dark and at death, her body became very small. Her friend Pema Yangkyi took Rainbow Body in 1911.

One of the methods used in Dzogchen to refine the gross elements of the body, reducing dependence on food and leading to Rainbow Body, is the practice of *chüdlen*[fn2], which means literally 'taking in the essence of the elements', nourishing oneself on the essence of the elements, which is light. Many practitioners have been able to stay for a long time in retreat through practising *chüdlen*. Longchenpa, for example, lived for long periods eating only the tiniest amount of flour and some pills. An added benefit is that this practice rejuvenates the body and strengthens the energy.

MASTERS WHO ATTAINED RAINBOW BODY

'Deeming my body a corpse, even though I'm not dead,
Is a sign that I perceive the universe as a magical illusion.'[14]

Nyagla Padma Duddul was a great master who sustained himself for a number of years on *chüdlen* and his breath and did many dark retreats. At one time, he was in retreat for six years. For the first three years he sustained himself through his breath and lived only on a single *chüdlen* pill a day plus a small amount of water and for the following three years he survived on only tiny amounts of medicinal substances and honey. These practices were all preparation for Rainbow Body, which he attained in 1872, when he was 56 years old, around the time of a summer full moon. This fantastic event was witnessed by hundreds of people and has been recorded in a biography. There are also oral accounts by Changchub Dorje and Ayu Khandro, who were two of Nyagla Padma Duddul's chief students.

Foreseeing his death, Nyagla Padma Duddul called together all his main disciples and told them that he would shortly be dead. Once they were all assembled, he gave them teachings and transmissions which he had not previously given. For many days, they practised the feast offerings of *ganapuja*[fn3] together in order that any obstacles that existed between the master and his students, and between students, would be purified, as this would be a grave obstruction to taking Rainbow Body. When he felt the time was right for him to die, Nyagla Padma Duddul told his students and said he wanted to go to a nearby mountain where he had received many of his *terma*.

'His disciples implored him not to die, but he said that it was time, and that there was nothing to be done about it.'[15] He went to the mountain with his students and they pitched a small tent for him. At his request, they then sewed him into this tent. He asked them to leave him undisturbed for seven days. The students went to the foot of the mountain and practised *guru yoga* and performed *ganapujas*, as Nyagla Padma Duddul had requested. During this period, there was heavy rain but many rainbows adorned the mountainside. After a week, on the morning of the eighth day, the students went back up the mountain. Opening up the tent, they found that there was no body there:

'All that they found inside was the master's clothes, his hair, and his fingernails and toenails. His clothes were the clothes of a lay person, and they remained there in a heap where he had been sitting, with the belt still wrapped around the middle. He had left them just like a snake sheds a skin.' [16]

Grief-stricken, the students called out Nyagla Padma Duddul's name and at that moment rainbow light appeared before them.

OTHER PRACTITIONERS WHO ATTAINED RAINBOW BODY

A number of people, including the brother of Jamgon Kongtrul, the great non-sectarian master of the nineteenth century, and Jamyang Khyentse Wangpo, once witnessed an elderly nun take Rainbow Body in a cowshed. While travelling around on pilgrimage, she had asked a wealthy family if she could use one of their cowsheds for a retreat, saying that she only needed it for one week. No one knew how she was going to eat, presuming she had made her own arrangements. She simply said that she wanted to do a closed retreat with the door of the shed sealed.

After only three days, shining 'swirling light-rays of different colours were seeping out of the holes and cracks of the cow shed's stone wall. Light was shining out from under the roof; while outside the shed, spheres of light moved rapidly about.' [17] No one knew if the nun was eating or drinking, for no one was bringing her food, nor was there any way to cook in the shed, as there was no fireplace. Before a week was up, wondering what was happening, the servants of the household forced open her door. Inside was the body of the nun, now 'fallen to pieces. Her hands were lying in one place and her feet were lying in another; her limbs were no longer connected to the body, but lay scattered in pieces. From the end of the bones, swirls of rainbow light were coiling out as the body continued to fall apart.'[18]

Fortunately someone realized that something marvellous was happening and made sure the cowshed was sealed again for the full seven days, as the nun had requested. At the end of that time there were no bones or parts of the nun's body littered about the shed nor any streaming rainbow light. Only nails and hair were left.

During the 1950s in eastern Tibet, a simple humble old man, a stonecarver, took Rainbow Body, to everyone's astonishment. No one even knew that he was a practitioner, although rumour had it that when he was young, and a hunter, he had received teachings from a great lama. Formerly a servant in a rich family, he earned a minimal living carving mantra into rocks. By day he worked and at night, save for two or three hours' sleep, he was in a state of contemplation. Not understanding that his father was actually integrating meditation with daily life, his son, who was a monk, felt that he should practise in a more formal and structured way. To this the stonecarver simply responded, 'Intrinsic wakefulness is the main point, my son. Simply try to maintain lucid awareness of intrinsic awareness itself, the natural state of being. There is no other Buddha.'[19]

A few years before he actually died, the stonecarver fell ill, but instead of becoming depressed, he became more and more joyful, composing his own songs of praise rather than singing traditional chants. He seemed to abandon all traditional Tibetan mantra, rituals or prayers, to the despair of his son, who was now convinced that his father had completely lost contact with the Buddhist teachings. But in response to his son's urgings, the old stonecarver replied, 'There is no external Buddha worth worshipping. The innate wakefulness of intrinsic awareness is one's primordial nature.'[20]

As his conditioned worsened, the old man addressed his son: 'Son, I have forgotten religion. Anyway, there is nothing to remember! All is illusory, yet I am happy – everything is perfect!'[21] His only request, as death approached, was that his body not be moved for a week.

At death, his corpse was dressed in his own clothes and kept in the house. Lamas and monks came to say ritual prayers for him and noticed on the sixth day that the old man, who had been tall, now seemed to be shrinking. Rainbow light was seen around the house[fn4]. On the day of his cremation, the eighth day, the undertakers came for his body, but inside his shroud there was nothing but nails and hair. The old man, unknown to everyone as a Dzogchen practitioner, had attained the supreme realization of Rainbow Body. The uncle of Chögyal Namkhai Norbu, Ogyen Tendzin, witnessed this himself, as did several people from different Buddhist schools as well as the Chinese government.

Togden Ogyen Tendzin, also manifested Rainbow Body. He had suffered from mental illness earlier on his life but had overcome this, mainly through the blessings of his teacher, Adzam Drugpa, and also by diligently practising Yantra Yoga and Chöd. In the light of his earlier difficulties, it was even more miraculous that he attained this level of realization. During the Cultural Revolution, he had been forced to come out of his isolated retreat in a cave. At that time being in retreat, 'not working', was considered parasitic. In fact religious practice of any kind was forbidden. Ogyen Tendzin was fortunate in that he was only placed under house arrest in a small wooden town house owned by Tibetans. There he was able to stay in retreat and was helped with provisions. Later he moved to the country, where a Tibetan official who had acted as a kind of guarantor for him checked up on him at regular intervals. On one of his visits, he found the house locked. There was no reply when he knocked and he was forced to break down the door.

'[He] found Togden's body on his meditation couch; but the body had shrunk to the size of that of a small child. The official was very worried: how was he to explain such a thing to his Chinese superiors? He was afraid they would probably believe that he was aiding Togden's escape in some way, and so went at once to inform them of what had happened.'[22]

When he returned to the house with Chinese government officials to look for the small body, they found nothing there, only hair and fingernails. Ogyen Tendzin had taken Rainbow Body, to the complete mystification of the Chinese. The Tibetan official, however, had some understanding of this phenomenon, saying that 'he had heard that ancient texts spoke about yogis realizing what was called a "Body of Light", although he had never expected to see such a thing himself'.[23]

Afraid of repercussions, he then escaped to Nepal and subsequently became a devoted practitioner, inspired by what he had been privileged to witness. In 1984 he met Chögyal Namkhai Norbu, to whom he told this story. Chögyal Namkhai Norbu said:

'I was deeply moved to hear of my uncle's realization. Knowing how serious a problem he had had with various mental disturbances in

his early life, I did not expect him to achieve so much in one life-
time. His example shows what is possible for every individual.[24]

MASTERS WHO CHOSE NOT TO TAKE RAINBOW BODY

There are also masters who have the capacity to take Rainbow
Body but do not do so because they have large numbers of students. Through their great compassion, they leave relics instead,
which transmit blessings through their physical presence.

One such master was Zhangtong, who lived in the eleventh
century. Without so many disciples, he said, his body would
have vanished completely at death. In his lifetime, he never cast
a shadow, a phenomenon known as *zangtal*[fn5], one of the signs
of having attained Rainbow Body. When he gave teachings on
Dzogchen, a rainbow tent would appear. This also appeared at
his death, accompanied by light, music and divine fragrance.

Another great master, a contemporary of the great yogi
Milarepa who chose not to dissolve his material body into rainbow light, was Dzeng Dharmabodhi. He also did not take
Rainbow Body because he 'continued to protect his disciples',[25]
even though he showed all the signs of complete mastery of
the elements. In life, his body was often seen veiled in rainbow
light and at death, the sky was filled with rainbows and he left
many relics.

A number of his students, however, including a nun and man
from eastern Tibet, a Khampa, did take Rainbow Body. There
were also 11 women who practised his instructions diligently and
whose bodies were enveloped with rainbow light at the time of
their death. Dzeng Dharmabodhi said that if anyone practised
his instructions 'for five or six years, with the care of a spinner

spinning wool, or of parents raising a sole surviving child, then his body will certainly vanish without a trace. He will leave no physical remains behind.'[26]

Dzeng Dharmabodhi's own teacher, Lama Bagom, left this world in a ball of light at the advanced age of 98. In turn he had received teachings from the great Dzogchen master Sherab Jungne, who had left in a blaze of rainbow light – after first hanging his robe, rosary and skullcup on a juniper tree!

THUGDAM

Amongst the Tibetans, there is also a way of dying whilst retaining consciousness through the process, known as *thugdam*. It is considered secondary to taking Rainbow Body.

Thugdam has been witnessed by many people in Tibet and Nepal over the centuries, but such accounts are frequently dismissed as folktales by Westerners, especially when the event happened many hundreds of years ago. However, a Western Dzogchen practitioner, Des Barry, who was staying at the Bonpo master Tenzin Namdak's monastery, Tritan Norbutse, in Nepal in December 1993, experienced *thugdam* at first hand. During his stay, he noticed that one of the elderly monks was very ill and was being helped around by his family. After a trip to Kathmandu, he returned to the monastery because he wanted to interview one of the young monks who had had a very dramatic journey over the Himalayas from Tibet to Nepal. But when he arrived back at Tritan Norbutse there was a lot of activity and the abbot, who was called Nyima, told him that he wouldn't be able to do the interview that day because the very old monk had just died that morning. Barry said how sorry he was to hear the news and the abbot replied:

'Yes, we too were sorry at first until we found out how he had died. We were doing a puja *in the morning and when it was over, all the monks stood up as usual, except the old monk, who was still seated in meditation posture. We thought that he was leaning against the back wall but when we went to lift him up, we found that he was not leaning against anything but had passed away whilst seated completely upright. Then we realized that he had died in* thugdam ...'[27]

They decided to carry out a kind of test to see if the old monk really had died in perfect thugdam, so they fetched a large black crown and put it on his head. Since the head and body still remained composed and upright, they knew that the monk's meditation was continuing beyond physical death. Nyima then asked Barry if he wanted to see the body. He would be allowed to do so as long as he didn't disturb anything. Barry had always been sceptical of such reports, since he had never witnessed anything of the sort before. They went down to the monastery, opened the door and went inside. The monk was still seated in perfect meditation posture.

'There was an amazing presence in the room, for although he was dead, there was a strong sensation of sharp clarity or consciousness present. [One of the monks wanted him to take a photograph, but he felt it was too invasive.] Afterwards, I felt very shocked by my experience for it had shaken my scepticism to the core. Then I thought to myself, "When I die, that is the way I would like to go." Being able to witness his manner of death was one of the most significant events in my life because I saw the actual results of meditation practice continue right into death and beyond ...'[28]

Altogether the old monk stayed in meditation posture for 36 hours after his death! A very unassuming person, with few possessions, whilst alive he hadn't given any real indications that he was a good practitioner at all. The Bonpo master Lopon Tenzin Namdak was very happy: 'Today a real Dzogchen practitioner died, not number one [meaning Rainbow Body style] but number two.'[29]

In *thugdam*, the period during which the body stays upright or maintains a fresh appearance after physical death varies according to the capacity of the practitioner. In the case of Tubthob Yeshe Togden, a Tibetan Rinpoche who died in July 1999, the period of *thugdam* lasted for 13 days. Lama Tenpai Nyima tells the story:

'Tubthob Yeshe Togden was a Gelugpa geshe who, after he had completed his studies in Sera monastery, spent over 30 years in retreat in a cave in the Himalayas. Later he became a teacher and divided his time between Dharamsala in India and the West, where he had several centres. Early in 1999, whilst he was staying in Dharamsala, he became ill and asked the Dalai Lama if he should travel to the West that year or not. The Dalai Lama told him that if his health improved a little he should go because the climate would be good for him. His health, however, continued to deteriorate whilst he was still in India until his condition became quite serious. He was suffering from acute oedema, but Tubthob was quite happy about it because he said that this was a good way to die [the body filling up with liquid can lead to a blissful death].

By July he was ready for death and asked to be taken to his mountain retreat. He asked his disciples to buy a clean white cloth with which to cover his body after he died. But his students didn't want him to die and were not certain that he couldn't recover from his illness. Rather than taking him to the mountains as he had requested, they decided to take him to hospital. On the journey, he asked his disciples where he was going. They told him that they were taking him home because they didn't want to tell him the truth! But when they arrived at the hospital gates, they discovered that Tubthob had already died. One of the doctors tried to resuscitate him on the spot but it was no use. Then his students knew that they had to get him to a place where he would not be disturbed, as quickly as possible. They drove straight back to his place in Dharamsala.

There he remained in the "lion's posture" for 13 days, during which time his lips remained bright red in colour and his skin and face took on a remarkable luminosity and clarity. In the morning, on the thirteenth day, several people said they saw a rainbow over his place although it was still virtually dark – around 3 or 4 a.m. The sky was also completely clear that morning, which is most unusual since it was during the monsoon when the sky is usually full of clouds. His body was burned later that day.'[30]

So long as the pure lineage of Dzogchen teachings continues and is practised precisely with diligence and devotion, the attainment of *thugdam* and Rainbow Body is not a myth and will continue now and into the future.

FOOTNOTES

[fn1] *Yangtig (yang thig)*: Quintessential method in Dzogchen.

[fn2] *Chüdlen* (Tib. *bchud len*), rasayana (Skt): Taking in the essence of the elements, which is one of the four practices for overcoming attachment; the use of long-life elixir prepared through the extraction of essential nutrients.

[fn3] Ganapuja is a Tantric ritual which involves the offering of meat and wine as well as other food. It is used to reaffirm the commitment between the disciple and the master as well as to heal any breaches between the disciples and put right any wrongdoing. Through this practice the practitioner can integrate their senses with the state of contemplation while eating and drinking.

[fn4] Accounts vary slightly over whether the old man was kept in a house or sewn up in a tent. According to Chögyal Namkhai Norbu, his uncle told him that it was in a tent.

[fn5] *Zangtal (zang thal)*: Direct, unobstructed transparent, unimpeded.

CHAPTER 12

TIBETAN BUDDHISM IN THE WEST

'Happy are those who know:
behind all words, the Unsayable stands;
and from the source, the Infinite
crosses over to gladness, and us.

Free of those bridges we raise
With constructed distinctions;
So that always, in each separate joy,
We gaze at the single, wholly mutual core.'[1]

It is now over three decades since the first Tibetan Buddhist teachers came to the West. Since then, the practice of 'Western Buddhism' has already undergone a substantial degree of development. The idealism of the early days has largely given way to a more pragmatic approach as many practitioners have realized that the real challenge with which they are faced is how to integrate their understanding into their own culture and everyday lives.

'To choose the Dharma never has and never can occur outside a cultural context ... As a European, I cannot step outside the history of which I am a creature.'[2]

Western ideas about the nature of spirituality are naturally conditioned by cultural history and specifically by religious heritage. Christian values still underpin our contemporary moral outlook, although our pagan roots are apparent in many of our traditional rituals and customs. Our technological and scientific sophistication, advanced intellectual and academic standards, together with our democratically based social system, present a very different soil for the Buddhist teachings to take root in compared to ancient India, Japan or Tibet.

Nevertheless, if we delve a little deeper, we find that many of the principles underlying Western esoteric approaches, such as gnosticism or alchemy, have much in common with traditional Buddhist thought. Modern physics too, as expounded by Fritjof Capra in *The Tao of Physics*, shows that the ideas of modern science and ancient mysticism are not unfamiliar to one another:

'In modern physics , the universe is thus experienced as a dynamic, inseparable whole which always includes the observer in an essential way. In this experience, the traditional concepts of space and time, of isolated objects, and of cause and effect lose their meaning. Such an experience, however, is very similar to that of the Eastern mystics.' [3]

At best, what is being offered at this time is the opportunity to combine the quintessence of the genuine spiritual expertise of the East with the very real material, scientific and educational advantages of the West, in a refined and discriminating manner.

A VISION OF TOTALITY

'To study the Dharma means to study oneself,
To study oneself means to forget oneself,
To forget oneself means to study the universe,
All excellence originates with introspection.'[4]

Self-observation or reflection is not generally highly esteemed as a quality within the context of our society at large. To be a responsible member of the community in the West implies being active in working and helping others within a political, sociological or economic context. Yet our own peace of mind and the ability to develop a sense of stability and trust within our intimate and family relationships are truly the foundations of our society. If we can start by respecting and understanding ourselves as well as those who are close to us, then we can progress both in terms of our own evolution and the development of society at large.

'Peace will not come if there is no evolution of the individual – for evolution means understanding that other people have needs just like me. This is the way to peace – the way is individual by individual. One may think, "When will that ever happen?" Yet our children will continue in the future. If I have an evolution [of consciousness] then I can help others who come after me. Thus, if it is not immediate, it is the genuine way forward in the long term. If each of us experiences an evolution then slowly we can have an effect on society. This is part of our awareness.'[5]

Taking a long-term view is important not only because it is more sustainable but also because it means that in the present moment, every individual counts. Changing society seems an overwhelming concept – the only real way is to start with ourselves. Rather than always directing our gaze outside, if we really want to do something significant we must first look within.

Since Dzogchen offers a direct path to self-knowledge which is free of religious constraints and cultural limitations as well as presenting a sharp tool for self-reflection which can help to cut through mental confusion and emotional or physical distress, it is a particularly useful approach at this critical time. On a more profound level, it tackles the very root of suffering, which is based on our dualistic vision.

THE CULTURAL CONTEXT

'Buddhism is not something which must be done only in a single way, mechanically following a given tradition, like that of Tibet or some other country. It's not like that. Its principal value goes beyond any one tradition.'[6]

Since the advent of Buddhism in the West, there has been a tendency to confuse the cultural attributes of the tradition with the spiritual path itself. This has been the source of a great deal of misunderstanding. The process of trying to substitute one ideology and culture for another, condemning Western values whilst over-idealizing the Oriental approach, is to make the mistake of 'throwing the baby out with the bathwater'. It is both unrealistic and counter-productive. To simply try to transport Buddhism, with all its cultural attributes, into a Western context is to make a serious error. Ultimately such an attitude leads to difficulties in integrating one's practice into daily life and means that the essence of the Buddhist teachings have not (and cannot) really take root. On the contrary, it is of fundamental importance for Westerners to be able to assimilate and integrate the teachings into their *own* culture in order to be able to communicate them to other Westerners in a genuine way.

The Dalai Lama, the political and spiritual leader of the Tibetan people, who is renowned for his openness, tolerance and simplicity of approach, places the inherent qualities of our common humanity above that of the more formal religious approaches since 'religious belief is no guarantee of moral integrity'.[7] Further:

'I believe there is an important distinction to be made between religion and spirituality. Religion I take to be concerned with belief in the claims to salvation of one faith or another ... Spirituality I take to be concerned with those qualities of the human spirit – such as love and compassion, patience, tolerance, forgiveness, contentment, a sense of responsibility, a sense of harmony – which bring happiness to self and others.'[8]

There is no doubt that Buddhist ideas, which embody such qualities as compassion, tolerance and forgiveness and are compatible with modern concepts of individuality, democracy and freedom of expression, are steadily attracting interest, especially in Europe and America.

'American Buddhism is hammering out its own shape: an emphasis on householder instead of monk, community instead of monastery, and a practice that integrates and makes use of all aspects of life, for all people, women as well as men.'[9]

Buddhism is redefining itself in different cultural contexts and integrating with local communities not only in North America but also in Europe, Australasia, South America and elsewhere.

Clearly, one of the factors which has made Buddhism, but especially Dzogchen, so appealing to the Western mind is its relative freedom from dogma, its insistence on individual enquiry into the nature of the mind and its emphasis on direct spiritual experience. It follows, of course, that if one reserves the right to discover the truth for oneself, one must also accord that same right to everyone else. This freedom of thought which naturally implies a respect for other faiths reflects a basic humanitarian tolerance which our world, made more intimate by our global connectedness, needs so acutely today.

'Living continuity requires both change and constancy... The survival of Buddhism today is dependent on its continuing ability to adapt. There is no inherent reason why a tradition that in the past has succeeded in travelling from India to Japan cannot make a similar transition to the countries of Europe ... the practice of Dharma is only meaningful if a significant transformation is effected within the practitioner.' [10]

There is, however, a very real danger that as this ancient teaching becomes ever more widespread and even 'fashionable' its quintessential meaning will be diluted and the teaching lineage abused. To maintain the purity of a living transmission in a time of change requires careful preservation of its integrity and essence in a dynamic way. This can only be effected within individuals who have experienced an inner realization of this essence directly – it cannot be effected simply through theoretical application or intellectual knowledge.

When the Buddhist path has become fully integrated within the Western lifestyle then that transition will have been accomplished. As the Dalai Lama says:

'As far as the teaching aspect is concerned it will always remain the same because the origin is the same. But the cultural aspect changes. Now you see Buddhism comes West. Eventually, it will be Western Buddhism.'[11]

That the role of the West is very significant in the continuation of the teachings has been recognized by many contemporary Tibetan teachers. The young Karmapa mentions America specifically in his prayer of aspiration for the future of Buddhism:

'... May the well-being of a golden age arise
In this realm of the thousand-petalled lotus.
May this time of warfare and disputation be pacified,
May auspicious excellence, prosperity and goodness
    flourish
Especially throughout the land of America.
May the youthful lotus of teaching and practice
    bloom.
May innumerable oceans of realms be filled
With the melodious roar of the profound secret.'[12]

THE FUTURE OF DZOGCHEN

While still a young man in Tibet, Chögyal Namkhai Norbu foresaw in a dream that his future lay in the West and that he would have many Western Dzogchen students. H.H. Dudjom Rinpoche predicted that many *terma* will be discovered in the West and will be aimed specifically at the Western mind and our contemporary circumstances. The *terma* tradition is one of the principal ways in which the Buddhist teachings, including the Dzogchen lineage, has maintained its freshness of approach over the centuries and has helped ensure that the lineage has always remained intact. There is, however, a possibility that too much emphasis may come to be placed on this tradition. There is even a danger that communities may form around modern *terma* teachings which in themselves are not sufficient to continue the pure total transmission of Dzogchen for future practitioners. Today, as in the future, it is vital that serious Dzogchen masters and practitioners return to the study and practice of the original teachings of Garab Dorje, the source of this lineage.

There is also the danger that in the course of time, the Dzogchen lineage will become diluted by Westerners or 'polluted' in the hands of unscrupulous teachers. Due to its fashionable status, Dzogchen is particularly susceptible to this type of abuse:

'The word "Dzogchen" will continue to be a good advertising tool for many teachers who want to attract students into their dharma *businesses. Because Dzogchen is revered by many as a high secret teaching, confused masters can easily learn a few technical buzzwords and tantric rituals to fool themselves and innocent practitioners. Although there will be many practitioners sincerely interested in Dzogchen knowledge, there may be very few masters who will be able to transmit this knowledge in a complete way... Confused masters and practitioners will change the original Dzogchen teachings to correspond to the sectarian principles of their religious institutions. People will water down the transmission by mistakenly setting up their "Dzogchen" systems to defend against others, even though Dzogchen is totally beyond logic and analysis.'*[13]

Yet, although this degenerate age is known as the Kali Yuga, the Dzogchen tradition has always managed to survive times of difficulty due to its quintessential nature. It has remained intact for thousands of years and will continue to do so …

May all beings recognize their own true nature and realize that *samsara* is the state of enlightenment. May many fortunate practitioners learn how to study, practise and integrate the pure and complete Dzogchen teachings into their lives. May Dzogchen knowledge continue to spread throughout the universe as envisioned by Guru Padmasambhava in his beautiful invocation:

'*May the unsurpassable Dzogchen teaching which is the secret treasure of all the Victorious Ones spread into the entire universe just like the sun illuminates the sky.*'

REFERENCES

Chapter 1

1. Chögyal Namkhai Norbu, *Dzogchen: The Self-Perfected State*, Arkana, 1989, p.3
2. Ibid., p.6
3. Nyoshul Khenpo, *Natural Great Perfection*, trans. Surya Das, Snow Lion Publications, 1995, p.90
4. Chögyal Namkhai Norbu, *The Crystal and the Way of Light*, ed. John Shane, Snow Lion Publications, 2000, p.11
5. Tulku Urgyen Rinpoche
6. Chögyal Namkhai Norbu, *The Crystal and the Way of Light*, op. cit., p.10, teaching retreat transcript.
7. Chögyal Namkhai Norbu, Samso, two teaching retreat transcripts in two volumes (vol. I: Conway, East coast USA, 1982; *see* Bibliography), p.128.
8. Chögyal Namkhai Norbu, California, 1979, transcript, vol. II, p.8
9. Chögyal Namkhai Norbu, Samso, op. cit., p.22
10. Chögyal Namkhai Norbu, California, op. cit., p.24
11. Ibid., p.51
12. Orally related story, Hampstead, June 2001
13. Surya Das, *The Snow Lion's Turquoise Mane*, HarperSan Francisco, 1992, p.17, teaching retreat transcript.
14. Chögyal Namkhai Norbu, Pomaia, Italy, January 1979, transcript trans. Barry Simmons, Snow Lion Publications, 1989, pp.131–2

15. Cited in Keith Dowman, *The Divine Madman*, Rider, 1980, p.55
16. Chögyal Namkhai Norbu, Pomaia, Italy, January 1979, transcript trans. Barry Simmons, Snow Lion Publications, 1989, p.100

Chapter 2

1. 'The Song of Realisation', *The Hundred Thousand Songs of Milarepa*, vol. I, p.133, trans. by Garma C. C. Chang, Shambhala, 1977
2. 'Sutta Nipata 1074' from *Reflections on the Life of the Buddha*, The Buddhist Society, 1983, p.22
3. Padmasambhava, *The Yoga of Knowing the Mind*, quoted in Chögyal Namkhai Norbu, *The Crystal and the Way of Light*, ed. John Shane, Routledge & Kegan Paul, 1986, p.89
4. Chögyal Namkhai Norbu, *The Crystal and the Way of Light*, ed. John Shane, Routledge & Kegan Paul, 1986, p.95
5. *The Lalitavistara sutra*
6. *The Prajnaparamita sutra*
7. Chögyal Namkhai Norbu, teaching transcript, December 1979, p.44
8. Quoted in 'Song of Mind' in Master Sheng Yen, *Poetry of Enlightenment*, Dharma Drum, New York, 1987, p.33
9. Chögyal Namkhai Norbu, London transcript, op. cit., p.376
10. Chögyal Trungpa, *Cutting through Spiritual Materialism*, 1973, p.218
11. Longchen Rabjam quoted in Tulku Thondup Rinpoche, *Buddha Mind*, Shambhala, p.ix
12. Chögyal Namkhai Norbu, Pomaia, Italy, January 1979, transcript trans. Barry Simmons, Snow Lion Publications, 1989, p.96
13. Chögyal Namkhai Norbu, Pomaia, Italy, January 1979, transcript trans. Barry Simmons, Snow Lion Publications, 1989, p.96
14. Chögyal Namkhai Norbu, *From the Depth of my Heart to my Mother*, Shang Shung Edizioni, Italy, 1995, p.15

Chapter 3

1. Nalanda, 1980, p.84, quoted in John Welwood, *Awakening the Heart: East /West Approaches to Psychotherapy and the Healing Relationship*, New Science Library, Shambhala, 1983
2. Chögyal Namkhai Norbu, Pomaia, Italy, January 1979, transcript trans. Barry Simmons, Snow Lion Publications, 1989, p.98

3. Chögyal Namkhai Norbu, *Direct Introduction to the State of Ati*, Shang Shung Edizioni, Italy, 1999, p.49
4. Chögyal Namkhai Norbu, T*he Crystal and the Way of Light*, ed. John Shane, Routledge & Kegan Paul, 1986, p.90
5. Chögyal Namkhai Norbu, quoted in Welwood, *see above.*
6. Chögyal Namkhai Norbu, *The Crystal and the Way of Light*, ed. John Shane, Snow Lion Publications, 2000, p.150
7. Chögyal Namkhai Norbu, teaching transcript notes, Merigar, Italy, 1995
8. Unpublished translation by Ossian MacLise (Sangye Nyenpa) of *The Treasure Chest of the Most Precious Expansiveness of Phenomena and so Forth*, Chapter One, p.3
9. Ibid.
10. Chögyal Namkhai Norbu, teaching transcript notes, Merigar, Italy, 1995
11. The last of 'The Six Vajra Verses', paraphrased from the original
12. Urgyen Tulku, *Rainbow Painting*, op. cit., p.173
13. John Welwood, 'Reflection and Presence: The Dialectic of Self-Knowledge', *Journal of Transpersonal Psychology* 1996, vol. 28, no. 2, p.109
14. Ibid., p.120
15. Harvey Cox, *Turning East*, Routledge, 1977, p.75
16. Chögyam Trungpa, 'Becoming a Full Human Being' in *Awakening the Heart*, Shambhala, 1983, p.127

Chapter 4

1. Chögyal Namkhai Norbu, *Dzogchen: The Self-Perfected State*, Arkana, 1989, p.3
2. Ani Tenzin Palmo, interview with B. Beresford, *U.K. Dzogchen Community Newsletter*, Spring 1992, p.42
3. Chögyal Namkhai Norbu, CD *Insegnamenti*, trans. Barrie Simmons, Rome, November 2000, Comunita Dzogchen, Rome
4. Tulku Urgyen Rinpoche, *Rainbow Painting*, Rangjung Yeshe Publications, 1995, p.35
5. Chögyal Namkhai Norbu, teaching transcript, London, December 1979 (as before), p.48
6. From 'The Song of the Vajra', quoted in Chögyal Namkhai Norbu,

The Crystal and the Way of Light, ed. John Shane, Routledge & Kegan Paul, 1986, p.91

7. Chögyal Namkhai Norbu, teaching transcript, Samso, Denmark, 1984, p.37

8. Chögyal Namkhai Norbu, Dzogchen: The Self-Perfected State, op. cit., p.7

9. Quoted in Urgyen Tulku, op. cit., p.189

10. Chögyal Namkhai Norbu, 'Awareness as Practice in Daily Life', The Mirror, issue 56, March 2001, p.2

11. Unpublished translation by Ossian MacLise (Sangye Nyenpa) of The Treasure Chest of the Most Precious Expansiveness of Phenomena and so Forth, Chapter One, p.4

12. Chögyal Namkhai Norbu, The Mirror, op. cit., p.2

13. Chögyal Namkhai Norbu, teaching transcript, Samso, Denmark, 1984, p.86

14. Tulku Urgyen Rinpoche, Vajra Speech, Rangjung Yeshe Publications, 2001, p.173

15. Nyoshul Khenpo, Natural Great Perfection, trans. Surya Das, Snow Lion Publications, 1995, p.75

16. Vajra speech, op. cit., p.131

17. James Low, Simply Being, Durtro Press, 1994, p.x

18. Chögyal Namkhai Norbu, London, December 1979 (as before), p.104

19. Khenpo Ngawang Palzang

20. Jigme Lingpa

21. Chögyal Namkahi Norbu, London transcript, 1979, p.104

22. Manjushri-namasamgiti Tantra

23. Julia Lawless and Judith Allan, 'Milarepa: The Great Magician', mss

Chapter 5

1. Nyoshul Khenpo, Natural Great Perfection, trans. Surya Das, Snow Lion Publications, 1995, p.58

2. Nagarjuna, quoted in Judith Simmer-Brown, Dakini's Warm Breath, Shambhala, 2001, p.81

3. Patrul Rinpoche, The Words of My Perfect Teacher: Kunzang Lama'i Shelung, HarperCollinsPublishers, 1997, p.xxxviii

4. Ibid.

5. Teaching given by Chögyal Namkhai Norbu at Lhatse, Tibet,

August 1988, *Dzogchen Community News*, West Coast of America, Summer 1989

6. Chögyal Namkhai Norbu, Kathmandu, Nepal, 1 January 1984, Richard Dixey transcription, p.143
7. Patrul Rinpoche, op. cit., p.138
8. Article by H.H. The Dalai Lama, *The Times of India*, 3 December 1992
9. Quoted in Matthieu Ricard, *Journey to Enlightenment*, Aperture, 1996, p.54
10. H.H. The Dalai Lama, *Dzogchen*, Snow Lion Publications, 2000, p.35
11. Chögyal Namkhai Norbu, Kathmandu, op. cit., p.143
12. Patrul Rinpoche, op. cit., p.35
13. Chögyal Namkhai Norbu, Conway, USA, July 1982 and January 1983, transcript
14. Ibid.
15. Vicki Mackenzie, *Cave in the Snow*, Bloomsbury, 1998, p.43
16. Julia Lawless and Judith Allan, 'Milarepa: The Great Magician', mss
17. Patrul Rinpoche, *The Words of My Perfect Teacher: Kunzang Lama'i Shelung*, HarperCollins*Publishers*, 1997, p.310
18. Quoted ibid., p. 312
19. Ibid.
20. Surya Das, *The Snow Lion's Turquoise Mane*, HarperSanFrancisco, 1992, p.155
21. Chögyal Namkhai Norbu, Conway, op. cit.
22. Chögyal Namkhai Norbu, *Dzogchen: The Self-Perfected State*, Arkana, 1989, p.36
23. Chögyal Namkhai Norbu, Conway, op. cit.
24. Chögyal Namkhai Norbu, *The Crystal and the Way of Light*, ed. John Shane, Snow Lion Publications, 2000, p.37
25. Ibid.
26. Chögyal Namkhai Norbu, London, December 1979, transcript
27. Quoted in Nyoshul Khenpo, *Natural Great Perfection*, trans. Surya Das, Snow Lion Publications, 1995, p.66
28. Chögyal Namkhai Norbu and Adriano Clemente, *Chogyal Namkhai Norbu: The Supreme Source*, Snow Lion Publications, 1999, p.20
29. Chögyal Namkhai Norbu, London, April 1979, transcript, p.30
30. Chögyal Namkhai Norbu, Pomaia, Italy, January 1979, transcript trans. Barry Simmons, p.103

Chapter 6

1. Chögyal Namkhai Norbu, Pomaia, Italy, January 1979, transcript trans. Barry Simmons
2. Chögyal Namkhai Norbu, California, 1979, transcript
3. Chögyal Namkhai Norbu, Conway, USA, July 1982 and January 1983, transcript
4. Chögyal Namkhai Norbu, *Dzogchen Ritual Practices*, Kailash Editions, 1991, p.51
5. Chögyal Namkhai Norbu, Pomaia, op. cit., p.29
6. Chögyal Namkhai Norbu, California, 1980, transcript
7. John Myrdhin Reynolds, *The Golden Letters*, Snow Lion Publications, 1996, p.69
8. Chögyal Namkhai Norbu, California, 1980, op. cit.
9. Chögyal Namkhai Norbu, California, 1979, op. cit.
10. Surya Das, *The Snow Lion's Turquoise Mane*, HarperSanFrancisco, 1992, pp.54 and 55
11. Ibid.
12. Chögyal Namkhai Norbu, California, 1979, op. cit.
13. Nyoshul Khenpo, *Natural Great Perfection*, trans. Surya Das, Snow Lion Publications, 1995, p.157
14. Ibid., p.179

Chapter 7

1. Tulku Thondup, *Masters of Meditation and Miracles*, Shambhala, 1996, p.59
2. Patrul Rinpoche, *The Words of My Perfect Teacher: Kunzang Lama'i Shelung*, HarperCollins*Publishers*, 1997, p. 338
3. Ibid., p.339
4. Tulku Tsewang, Jamyang and L. Tashi, *Longchenpa's Great History of the Innermost Essence of Dzogchen*, vol. IX of the *Nyingthig Yazhi*, New Delhi, 1971, trans. Dr Jim Valby, pp.84–165
5. Chögyal Namkhai Norbu and Adriano Clemente, *The Supreme Source*, Snow Lion Publications, 1999, pp.26 and 27
6. H.H. The Dalai Lama, *Dzogchen*, Snow Lion Publications, 2000, p.42
7. Tsewang, Jamyang and Tashi, op. cit.
8. Patrul Rinpoche, op. cit., p.339
9. Ibid., p. 340

10. Tsewang, Jamyang and Tashi, op. cit.
11. 'Sutra of Final Nirvana', quoted in Dudjom Rinpoche, *The Nyingma School of Tibetan Buddhism*, vol. I, Wisdom Publications, 1991, p.746
12. Tulku Thondup, *Masters of Meditation and Miracles*, Shambhala, 1996, p.77
13. Ibid., p.79
14. Dudjom Rinpoche, op. cit., p.513
15. Tulku Thondup, op. cit., p.84
16. Ibid.
17. Ibid., p.90
18. Ibid., p.91
19. *The Lives and Liberation of Princess Mandarava*, trans. Lama Chonam and Sangye Khandro, Wisdom Publications, 1998, p.87
20. Ibid., p.137
21. Ibid., p.178
22. Ibid., p.192
23. *Masters of the Nyingma Lineage*, Crystal Mirror series, vol. II, Dharma Publishing, 1995, p.33
24. Norma Levine, *Blessing Power of the Buddhas*, Element Books, 1993, p.48
25. Ibid.

Chapter 8

1. Jigme Lingpa, quoted in Tulku Thondup, *Masters of Meditation and Miracles*, Shambhala, 1996, pp.124–5
2. Dudjom Rinpoche, *The Nyingma School of Tibetan Buddhism*, vol. I, Wisdom Publications, 1991, p.577
3. Quoted ibid,. p.579
4. Quoted in Tulku Thondup, op. cit, p.114
5. Dudjom Rinpoche, op. cit., p.837
6. Tulku Thondup, op. cit., p.123
7. Quoted ibid., p.132
8. Quoted in Surya Das, *The Snow Lion's Turquoise Mane*, HarperSanFrancisco, 1992, p.21
9. Quoted in Tulku Thondup, op. cit., p.204
10. Quoted ibid, p.208
11. 'The Song of Energy' in *Tara Mandala* newsletter, Spring 1996, p.9

12. Quoted in Matthieu Ricard, *Journey to Enlightenment*, Aperture, 1996, p.14

13. Lhundrub Tso, *A Brief Biography of Adzam Drugpa*, Shang-Shung Edizioni, 1993, p.14

14. Quoted in Tsultrim Allione, *Women of Wisdom*, Arkana, 1984, p.241

15. Ibid, p.252

16. Quoted ibid., p.237

Chapter 9

1. Prophecy from the treasures of Trime Kunga (*dri med kun dga'i gter lung*), quoted in Dudjom Rinpoche, *The Nyingma School of Tibetan Buddhism*, vol. I, Wisdom Publications, 1991, p.935

2. Nyoshul Khenpo, *Natural Great Perfection*, Snow Lion Publications, 1995, p.180

3. Quoted in Norma Levine, *Blessing Power of the Buddhas*, Element Books, 1993, p.45

4. Quoted in Dudjom Rinpoche, *The Nyingma School of Tibetan Buddhism*, vol. I, Wisdom Publications, 1991, p.749

5. Tulku Thondup Rinpoche, *Hidden Teachings of Tibet*, Wisdom Publications, 1986, p.62

6. Ibid., p.78

7. Matthieu Ricard, *Journey to Enlightenment*, Aperture, 1996, p.41

8. Quoted ibid.

9. Surya Das, *The Snow Lion's Turquoise Mane*, HarperSanFrancisco, 1992, p.182

10. Dudjom Rinpoche, *The Nyingma School of Tibetan Buddhism*, vol. I, Wisdom Publications, 1991, p.770

11. Tulku Thondup Rinpoche, op. cit., p.78

12. Dudjom Rinpoche, op. cit., p. 840

13. Surya Das, op. cit., p.73

14. Quoted in Tulku Thondup Rinpoche, op. cit., p.219

15. Chögyal Namkhai Norbu, *The Practice of the Long Life of the Immortal Dakini Mandarava*, Shang Shung Edizioni, 1999, p.18

16. Oral account by Chögyal Namkhai Norbu at Kunselling, Wales, November 1998, Richard Dixey transcription

17. Ibid.

18. Ibid.

Chapter 10

1. Carl Jung, 1976; *see The Sacred Heritage*, Routledge, 1997, p.13, para 591
2. Julia Lawless and Judith Allan, 'Milarepa: the Great Magician', mss
3. Ibid.
4. Ibid.
5. Quoted in Tenzin Wangyal Rinpoche, *The Tibetan Yogas of Dream and Sleep*, Snow Lion Publications, 1998, p.12
6. J. C. Neihardt, *Black Elk Speaks*, University of Nebraska Press, 1979, p.186
7. Kilton Stewart, *Dream Theory in Malaya*, research report from expedition in 1935 (publisher unknown), p.5
8. Chögyal Namkhai Norbu, *The Dream Work Book*, teachings compiled by Marianna Zwollo, Stichting Dzogchen, November 1987
9. Chögyal Namkhai Norbu, *Cycle of Day and Night*, Blue Dolphin Press, USA, 1984, p.48
10. Ibid.
11. Chögyal Namkhai Norbu, *Dream Yoga and the Practice of Natural Light*, ed. Michael Katz, Snow Lion Publications, 1992, p.47

Chapter 11

1. William Wordsworth, 'My Heart Leaps Up', *The Oxford Book of Nineteenth Century Verse*, chosen by John Hayward, Oxford University Press, 1964, p.61
2. John 20:9
3. Rainer Maria Rilke, 'Mary at Peace with the Risen Lord', *Selected Works*, vol. II, Hogarth Press, 1967, p.220
4. John 20:30
5. Notes from talks by Pir Vilayat Khan, Beauchamp Lodge, Warwick Crescent, London, December 2000
6. Ibid.
7. Ibid.
8. Chögyal Namkhai Norbu, *The Crystal and the Way of Light*, ed. John Shane, Snow Lion Publications, 2000, p.162
9. Ibid., pp.157–8
10. Tulku Thondup, *Masters of Meditation and Miracles*, Shambhala Publications, 1996, p.72
11. Dudjom Rinpoche, 'A Prayer by which to Recognise One's Own

Faults and Keep the Object of Refuge in Mind. A Very Pure Aspiration to be Absolutely Clear as to What to Adopt and What to Abandon', trans. Mike Dickman, unpublished

12. Ibid.
13. Dudjom Rinpoche, *The Nyingma School of Tibetan Buddhism*, vol. I, Wisdom Publications, 1991, p.540
14. Nyagla Padma Duddul, *Songs of Experience*, Shang Shung Edizioni, p.14
15. Chögyal Namkhai Norbu, op. cit., p.158
16. Ibid., p.159
17. Tulku Urgyen Rinpoche, *Rainbow Painting*, Rangjung Yeshe Publications, 1995, p.182
18. Ibid.
19. Surya Das, *The Snow Lion's Turquoise Mane*, HarperSanFrancisco, 1992, p.132
20. Ibid.
21. Ibid.
22. Chögyal Namkhai Norbu, *The Crystal and the Way of Light*, ed. John Shane, Snow Lion Publications, 2000, pp.160–1
23. Ibid., p.161
24. Ibid.
25. Dudjom Rinpoche, *The Nyingma School of Tibetan Buddhism*, vol. I, Wisdom Publications, 1991, p.550
26. Ibid., p.547
27. Oral account by Des Barry, Hampstead, London, July 2001
28. Ibid.
29. Ibid.
30. Oral account by Lama Tenpai Nyima, Hampstead, London, June 2001

Chapter 12

1. Rainer Maria Rilke from *Beneath a Single Moon*, Shambhala, 1991, p.152
2. Stephen Bachelor, *The Awakening of the West*, Aquarian, 1994, p.276
3. Fritjof Capra, *The Tao of Physics*, Fontana/Collins, 1975, p.86
4. Adzom Rinpoche, quoted in *The Dzogchen Newsletter*, December 2000, back cover

5. Chögyal Namkhai Norbu, CD *Insegnamenti*, trans. Barrie Simmons, Rome, November 2000, Comunita Dzogchen, Rome
6. Chögyal Namkhai Norbu, Pomaia, Italy, January 1979, transcript trans. Barry Simmons
7. The Dalai Lama, *Ancient Wisdom, Modern World*, Little, Brown and Company, 1999, p.22
8. Ibid.
9. Rick Fields, *How the Swans Came to the Lake*, Shambhala, 1992, p.380
10. Stephen Bachelor, op. cit., p.279
11. Quoted in *How the Swans Came to the Lake*, op. cit., p.379
12. Ugyen Trinley, the seventeenth Karmapa, from *A Feast for the Fortunate, A Lamp Aspiration!*, August 1999
13. Dr Jim Valby (Tibetan scholar and translator) from a piece written specifically for this book. Conway, USA, December 2002

GLOSSARY

Introduction
Dzogchen (*rdzogs chen*)
Tawa (*lta.ba.*)

Chapter 1: Dzogchen: The Great Perfection
Chögyal Namkhai Norbu (1938–) (*chos rgyal nam mkha'i nor bu*)
Drugpa Kunley (*'brug pa kun legs*) (1455–1529)
ngöndro (*sngon 'gro*)
Patrul Rinpoche (*dpal sprul rin po che*) (1808–1887) also known as
    rdza dpal sprul or *o rgyan 'jigs med chos kyi dbang po*

Chapter 2: The Buddha's Teachings
Naropa (*na ro pa*) (1016–1100)
Shunyata (*stong pa nyid*)
Tilopa (*til li pa*) (988–1069)
Vajra (*rdo.rje*)

Chapter 3: Mirror of the Mind
drebu (*'bras bu*)
lam (*lam*)
Longde (*klong sde*)
Semde (*sems sde*)
Upadesha (*man ngag sde*)
zhi (*gzhi*)

Chapter 4: The Practice of Meditation

chöd (*gcod*)
lhagthong (*lhag mthong*)
Machig Labdron (*Ma gcig lab sgron*) (1055–1153)
Milarepa (*mi la ras pa*) (1040–1123)
rigpa (*rig pa*)
shine (*zhi gnas*)
Yantra Yoga (*trulkhor*) (*'phrul 'khor*)

Chapter 5: The Value of an Authentic Teacher

Changchub Dorje (*byang chub rdo rje*)
Jigme Gyalwai Nyugu (*'jigs med rgyal ba'i myu gu*)
Jigme Lingpa (*'jigs med gling pa*)
Khamtrul Rinpoche (*khams sprul rin po che*)
Lama (*bla ma*)
Longchenpa (*klong chen pa*)
Marpa (*mar pa*) (1012–1097)
Milarepa (*mi la ras pa*) (1040–1123)
Nagarjuna (*klu grub*)
Padmasambhava (*pad ma 'byung gnas*)
Patrul Rinpoche (*dpal sprul rin po che*) (1808–1887)
Shantideva (*zhi ba lha*) (685–763)
Tsawai Lama (*rtsa ba'i bla ma*)
Tulku Ugyanpa (*sprul sku u rgyan pa*)

Chapter 6: Guru Yoga and Transmission

Dharmakaya (Skt) (Tib. *chos kyi sku*)
Do Khyentse Yeshe Dorje (*mdo mkhyen brtse ye shes rdo rje*) (1800–1859)
Garab Dorje (*dga' rab rdo rje*)
kama (*bka' ma*)
Manjusrimitra (*'jam dpal bshes gnyen*)
Naropa (*na ro pa*) (1016–1100)
Nirmanakaya (Skt) (Tib. *sprul pa'i sku*)
Samantabhadra (*kun tu bzang po*)
Samaya (Skt) (Tib. *damtsig, dam tshig*)
Samboghakaya (Skt) (Tib. *longs spyod rdzogs sku*)
terma (*gter ma*)
terton (*gter ston*)
Tilopa (*til li pa*) (988–1069)

Vajra (Skt.) (Tib. *rdo.rje*)
Vajrapani (*phyag na rdo rje*)
Yeshe Tsogyal (*ye shes mtsho rgyal*)

Chapter 7: Early Dzogchen Masters

Dra Thalgyur (*sgra thal 'gyur chen po'i rgyud*)
Garab Dorje (*dGa' rab rdo rje*)
Jnanasutra (*ye shes mdo*)
Longde (*klong sde*)
Manjusri (*'jam dpal*)
Manjusrimitra (*'jam dpal bshes gnyen*)
Rigdzin (*rig 'dzin*) (*Vidyadhara*)
Samboghakaya (Skt) (Tib. *longs sku, longs spyod rdzogs sku*)
Semde (*sems sde*)
Shangshung Nyengyüd (*zhang zhung snyan brgyud*)
Shenrab Miwoche (*gshen rab mi bo che*)
Tregchod (*khregs chod*)
Trisong Detsen (*Khri srong Lde'u bstan*)
Tsig sum ned dag (*tshig gsum gnad brdegs*)
Upadesha (*man ngag sde*)
Vairocana (*bai ro tsa na*)
Vidyadhara (or *Rigdzin*) (*rig 'dzin*)
Vimalamitra (*dri med bshes gnyen*)
Yeshe Tsogyal (*ye shes mtsho rgyal*)

Chapter 8: Later Lineage of Knowledge

Adzam Drugpa (*a 'dzam 'brug pa'*)
Avalokiteshvara (*spyan ras gzigs*)
Do Khyentse Yeshe Dorje (1800–1859)
Drigung Kagyu (*'bri gung bka' brgyud*)
Drugchen (*'brug chen*)
Jigme Gyalwai Nyugu (*'jigs med rgyal bai' myu gu*)
Jigme Lingpa (*'jigs med gling pa*)
Kongtrul Rinpoche/Jamgon Kongtrul Lodro Thaye (*'jam mgon kong sprul blo gros mtha'yas*) (1813–1890)
Kunzang Lama'i Shelung (*kun bzang bla ma'i zhal lung*)
Longchenpa (*klong chen pa*)
Lundrub Tso (*lhun grub tso*)
Nyagla Padma Duddul (*nyag bla pad ma bdud 'dul*)

rigpai tsal wang (*rig pa'i rtsal dbang*)

rime (*ris med*)

Sixteenth Karmapa (*rGyal ba Karmapa, Rangbyung rig pa'i rdo rje*) (1924–1981)

terton (*gter ston*)

Togdan (*rtogs ldan*)

tsampa (*tsam pa*)

Vajrayogini (Skt), Dorje Naljorma (Tib.) (*rdo rje rnal 'byor ma*)

Yangtig (*yang thig*)

Chapter 9: Visions and Terma

Dilgo Khyentse (*ldil mgo mkhyen brtse*) (1910–1991)

gong ter (*dgongs gter*)

Guru Chowang (*gu ru chos dbyang*) (1212–1270)

Kangkar Rinpoche (*Gangs dKar Rin po che*) (1903–1956)

Jamyang Chokyi Wangchug (*'Jam dbyangs Chos kyi dBang phyug*) (1910–1963)

Jamyang Khyentse Wangpo (*'ja, dbyangs mkhyen brtse dbang po*) (1820–1892)

Jomo Menmo (*jo mo sman mo*) (1248–1283)

Dorje Lingpa (*rdo rje gling pa*) (1346–1405)

Karma Lingpa (*bka' ma gling pa*) (1327–1387)

Ratna Lingpa (*rat na gling pa*) (1403–1478)

Sangye Lingpa (*sangs rgyas gling pa*) (1340–1396)

Terdag Lingpa (*gter bdag gling pa*) (1646–1714)

Mingyur Dorje (*mi 'gyur rdo rje*)

Rinchen Terdzöd (*rin chen gter mdzod*)

sa ter (*sa gter*)

terma (*gter ma*)

terton (*gter ston*)

Vajra Varahi (Skt.) Dorje Phagmo (Tib.) (*rdo rje phag mo*)

Chapter 10: Dreams and Death

bardo (*bar do*)

Shang Shung (*zhang zhung*)

tagdrol (*btag sgrol*)

Chapter 11: Realization and the Rainbow Body

jalü (*'ja' lus*)

jalü powa chenpo (*'ja' lus 'pho ba chen po*)

Nyagla Padma Duddul (*nyag bla pad ma bdud 'dul*)

Pang Mipham Gonpo (*spangs mi pham mgon po*)

Togden Ogyen Tendzin (*rtogs ldan o rgyan bstan 'dzin*)

Thigle (*thig.le*)

thugdam (*thugs dam*)

BIBLIOGRAPHY

Tsultrim Allione, *Women of Wisdom*, Arkana, 1984

Stephen Batchelor, *Awakening of the West*, Aquarian, 1994

Big Sky Mind: Buddhism and the Beat Generation, ed. Carole Tonkinson, Thorsons, 1995

Fritjof Capra, *The Tao of Physics*, Fontana/Collins, 1975

H.H. The Dalai Lama, article in *The Times of India*, 3 December 1992

H.H. The Dalai Lama, *Dzogchen*, Snow Lion Publications, 2000

H.H. The Dalai Lama, *Ancient Wisdom, Modern World*, Little, Brown and Company, 1999

Surya Das, *The Snow Lion's Turquoise Mane*, HarperSanFrancisco, 1992

Keith Dowman, *The Divine Madman*, Rider, 1980

Dudjom Rinpoche, *The Nyingma School of Tibetan Buddhism*, vol. I, Wisdom Publications, 1991

Nyagla Padma Duddul, *Songs of Experience*, Shang Shung Edizioni, Italy

Rick Fields, *How the Swans Came to the Lake*, Shambhala, 1992

Kent Johnson and Craig Paulenich, *Beneath a Single Moon: Buddhism in Contemporary American Poetry*, Shambhala, 1991

Nyoshul Khenpo, *Natural Great Perfection*, trans. Surya Das, Snow Lion Publications, 1995

Julia Lawless and Judith Allan, 'Milarepa: The Great Magician', mss

Norma Levine, *Blessing Power of the Buddhas*, Element Books, 1993

James Low, *Simply Being*, Durtro Press, 1994

Vicki Mackenzie, *Cave in the Snow*, Bloomsbury, 1998

Masters of the Nyingma Lineage, ed. Tarthang Tulku, Crystal Mirror series, vol. XI, Dharma Publishing, 1995

John Neihardt, *Black Elk Speaks*, University of Nebraska Press, 1979

Chögyal Namkhai Norbu, *The Cycle of Day and Night*, Blue Dolphin Press, USA, 1984

—, *The Dream Work Book*, teachings compiled by Marianna Zwollo, Stichting Dzogchen, 1987

—, *Dzogchen: The Self-Perfected State*, Arkana, 1989

—, Teaching given at Lhatse, Tibet, August 1988, *Dzogchen Community News*, West coast of America, Summer 1989

—, *Dzogchen Ritual Practices*, Kailash Editions, 1991

—, *Dream Yoga and the Practice of Natural Light*, ed. Michael Katz, Snow Lion Publications, 1992

—, *The Practice of the Long Life of the Immortal Dakini Mandarava*, Shang Shung Edizioni, 1999

—, *The Crystal and the Way of Light*, ed. John Shane, Routledge & Kegan Paul, 1986

Chögyal Namkhai Norbu and Adriano Clemente, *Chögyal Namkhai Norbu: The Supreme Source*, Snow Lion Publications, 1999

Notes from talks by Pir Vilayat Khan at Beauchamp Lodge, Warwick Crescent, London, December 2000

The One Hundred Thousand Songs of Milarepa, vols I and II, trans. Garma C. C. Chang, Shambhala, 1977

The Oxford Book of Nineteenth Century Verse, ed. John Hayward, Oxford University Press, 1964

Padmasambhava, *The Lives and Liberation of Princess Mandarava*, trans. Lama Chonam and Sangye Khandro, Wisdom Publications, Boston, 1998

Rainer Maria Rilke, *Selected Works*, vol. II, Hogarth Press

Patrul Rinpoche, *The Words of My Perfect Teacher: Kunzang Lama'i Shelung*, HarperCollins*Publishers*, 1994

John Myrdhin Reynolds, *The Golden Letters*, Snow Lion Publications, 1996

Matthieu Ricard, *Journey to Enlightenment*, Aperture, 1996

Judith Simmer-Brown, *Dakini's Warm Breath*, Shambhala, 2001

'The Song of Energy', *Tara Mandala* newsletter, Spring 1996

John Snelling, *The Buddhist Handbook*, Rider, 1986

Jamyang and L. Tashi, *Longchenpa's Great History of the Innermost*

Essence of Dzogchen, vol. IX, *Nyingthig Yazhi, Tulku Tsewang*, trans. Dr Jim Valby, New Delhi, 1971

Tulku Thondup Rinpoche, *Hidden Teachings of Tibet*, Wisdom Publications, 1986

—, *Masters of Meditation and Miracles*, Shambhala, 1996

Lhundrub Tso, *A Brief Biography of Adzam Drugpa*, Shang-Shung Edizioni, 1993

Tsoknyi Rinpoche, *Carefree Dignity*, Rangjung Yeshe Publications, 1998

Tulku Urgyen Rinpoche, *Rainbow Painting*, Rangjung Yeshe Publications, 1995

—, *Vajra Speech*, Rangjung Yeshe Publications, 2001

Tenzin Wangyal Rinpoche, *The Tibetan Yogas of Dream and Sleep*, Snow Lion Publications, 1998

John Welwood, *Awakening the Heart: East/West Approaches to Psychotherapy and the Healing Relationship*, New Science Library, Shambhala, 1983

Transcriptions of talks by Chögyal Namkhai Norbu:

Nepal, 1 January 1984, transcribed by Richard Dixey

Conway, USA, July 1982 and January 1983

California, 1979

London, April 1979

London, December 1979

Pomaia, Italy, January 1979

California, 1980

Samso, Denmark, 1984

Kunselling, Wales, November 1998, transcribed by Richard Dixey

BIOGRAPHY OF
CHÖGYAL NAMKHAI NORBU

Chögyal Namkhai Norbu was born in Tibet in 1938, where at the age of two he was recognized as the reincarnation of the great turn-of-the-century Dzogchen master Adzam Drugpa. In 1960 he was invited to Italy by the Tibetan scholar Prof. Tucci and subsequently worked for 30 years at Naples University, teaching Tibetan and Mongolian studies. He began teaching Dzogchen in the early 1970s and today is recognized as one of the principal contemporary Dzogchen masters, with thousands of students all over the world, collectively known as 'the Dzogchen community'. He is the author of many renowned books on Dzogchen as well as on Tibetan history and culture.

CONTACTS

Further contacts can be made in countries around the world through those noted below.

Argentina

Dzogchen Community South America
Tashigar, CC No. 25-5155, Tanti, Pcia de Cordoba, Argentina
Tel/Fax: 3541 498 884   e-mail: tashigar@dcc.com.ar

Australia

Dzogchen Community Australia
Namgyalgar, PO Box 14, Central Tilba, NSW 2546
Tel/Fax: 61 02 4473 7668   e-mail: namgyalg@acr.net.au

Rigpa Australia
12/37 Nicholson Street, Balmain, NSW 2041
Tel: 61(0)2 555 9952

India

Rigpa India
Rigpa House, RA46, Inderpuri, PO Pusa, New Delhi 12
Tel: 91 11 576 7882

Italy

Dzogchen Community Italy
Merigar Communita Dzogchen, Arcidosso 58031, GR
Tel: 39 0564 966 837   e-mail: merigaroffice@tiscalinet.it

Switzerland

Rigpa Switzerland
PO Box 253, 8059 Zurich
Tel: 41(0)1 463 33 53

Thailand

Dzogchen Community Thailand
Geoffrey Blake, 33 Soi Lang Suan-Ploenchit Road, Bangkok 10330
Tel: 66 2 2549061   e-mail: gblake@mozart.inet.co.th

United Kingdom

Dzogchen Community UK
Contact: Amely Becker, 15a Langdon Park Road, London N6 5PS
Tel: 020 8348 6253   e-mail: amely@globalnet.co.uk

Rigpa UK
330 Caledonian Road, London N1 1BB
Tel: 020 7700 0185

United States of America

Dzogchen Community North America
Tsegyalgar, PO Box 277, Conway, MA 01341, USA
Tel: (413) 369 4153   e-mail: DzogchenUSA@compuserve.com

Rigpa USA
PO Box 607, Santa Cruz, CA 95061-0607
Tel: 1(408) 454 9103

Rigpa Center, Berkeley
Tel: 1(510) 644 1858